PRAGUE
HIDDEN SPLENDORS

Marketa Theinhardt
Pascal Varejka

PRAGUE
HIDDEN SPLENDORS

Translated from the French by Deke Dusinberre

Photography by

Pavel Stecha

Flammarion

Paris - New York

Page 1:
Former royal waiting room of Prague's main train station
see page 76

Frontispiece:
The Estates Theater
see page 58

Page 6:
The Malá Strana quarter of Prague

Designed by François Abegg
Copyediting by Christine Schultz-Touge
and Bernard Wooding

Typesetting by P.F.C., Dole
Photoengraving by Pack Edit, Wasquehal
Printed by Clerc S. A., Saint-Amand-Montrond
Bound by Sirc, Marigny-le-Châtel

Flammarion
26, rue Racine
75006 Paris

ISBN: 2-08013-554-6
N° d'édition: 1129
Dépôt légal: March 1994

Printed in France

CONTENTS

INTRODUCTION

Most foreign visitors are struck by the beauty of Prague, a city that poet Rainer Maria Rilke once compared to a "rich, vast epic poem of architecture."

Travelers arriving in the Golden City are immediately impressed by the harmony of its stone houses and palaces, and by the pattern of its streets. Prague has been able to retain these traces of its past far longer than other cities due to a series of historical incidents. The loss of Bohemia's political independence and the transfer of the government to Vienna in the seventeenth century relegated Prague to the position of a provincial city during two centuries of Hapsburg rule. In the twentieth century, economic growth was completely stifled during Nazi occupation and the recent period of Communist rule.

Prague's history remains "written in the stone" of its Gothic and baroque monuments—the architectural styles that characterize the city. An eloquent symbol of this unique heritage, the Charles Bridge (Karlův most) was built in the fourteenth century during the reign of Charles IV, to which baroque statues were added in the late seventeenth and early eighteenth centuries.

Beyond initial impressions, however, the Golden City hides many other treasures. There is no room here to dwell on Prague's special ambience, on its magic atmosphere, or on its rich literary and musical associations—this volume focuses on architecture, particularly on interiors, both public and private. While the former are widely known, the latter are far less so. This is because tourists are either unaware of their existence or do not have the time to visit them. Some places will be familiar only to people who have actually lived in Prague. This book opens the doors to churches, castles, theaters, cafés, restaurants, shops, and office buildings, as well as to more intimate interiors such as artists' homes. The extraordinary richness of the city's architecture makes this tour a voyage through time.

The oldest description of Prague is by the Jewish merchant and diplomat from Andalusia, Ibrahim ibn-Ya'qub, who in 965 wrote of a "city built of stone and lime." Nothing remains of the pre-Romanesque town seen by Ibn-Ya'qub; Prague's oldest traces come from the Romanesque city built around Old Town Square (Staroměstské náměstí) and Little Square (Malé náměstí), and these vestiges now lie below street level. Dams and embankments were built in the mid-thirteenth century to forestall the flooding of the Vltava River, thereby raising the level of the ground. This explains why the oldest interiors of the city are now found in basements. One of the most interesting buildings from this standpoint is the House of the Lords of Kunštát (Dům pánů z Konštátu), where the underground level was once the ground floor of the original Romanesque edifice.

Prague Castle (Pražský hrad) also has several authentic Romanesque interiors, such as the hall in the palace of Přemyslid princes Soběslav I (1125–1140) and Vladislav II (1140–1172). The hall, some fifty yards long, is now at basement level, below the Gothic palace built by the rulers of the Jagiello and the Luxembourg dynasties. The church dedicated to St. George (sv. Jiří) also has a fine Romanesque crypt.

Vestiges of Gothic architecture are far more numerous. In fact, the basic structure of the city center is Gothic, built around six basic neighborhoods. On the right bank of the Vltava is Old Town (Staré Město), noted for a town hall with a crowd-pleasing astronomical clock, and for the church of Our Lady of Týn (Panna Marie před Týnem), the old Jewish quarter (Josefov), with its Old-New Synagogue, and New Town (Nové Město), founded by Charles IV in 1348. New Town has its own town hall and what was to have been the tallest church in Prague — St. Mary of the Snows (Panna Marie Sněžná). Only the nave was completed and the vaulted roof collapsed in the sixteenth century. Its baroque high altar, Prague's largest, is still intact.

Further south is High Castle (Vyšehrad), on a spot rich with legend since it was here that the princess and prophetess Libuše, mythical ancestor of Bohemia's first ruling dynasty, the Přemyslids, reportedly had her vision announcing the founding of Prague. On the left bank is the Hrad, or Prague Castle, (actually a royal city that includes the old palace, fortifications, and St. Vitus Cathedral, which was only completed in 1929), and finally Malá Strana (the "little quarter"), a neighborhood that is thoroughly baroque.

Gothic Prague has also retained its main thoroughfare, the Royal Road (králová cesta), which was followed when the kings of Bohemia were crowned. Traditionally, the coronation procession started at High Castle, entered Old Town through the Powder Tower gate (Prašná brána), crossed Old Town Square and took narrow, winding Charles Street (Karlova) to the bridge of the same name (proudly protected by a tower at each end), then made its way up to Prague Castle. As the names suggest, the golden age of Gothic Prague occurred during the reign of Charles IV of Luxembourg, king of Bohemia and Holy Roman Emperor, who ruled from 1346 to 1378. Charles founded central Europe's first university in Prague in 1348 and made the city the capital of his empire, spurring growth and development by erecting prestigious buildings.

Most Gothic churches, monasteries and convents were remodeled during the baroque era and have therefore lost their original interiors, with the exception of certain buildings such as St. Vitus Cathedral (katedrála svatého Víta) which, even though it took six hundred years to complete, displays an undeniable unity of style. Religious edifices with authentic Gothic interiors include the Old-New Synagogue (Staronová synagóga), the oldest synagogue in Europe. It was begun in 1270 and completed in 1275, a period of transition between the Romanesque and the Gothic styles, and has unusual five-ribbed vaulting. Also worth noting is the chapel of St. Wenceslas (sv. Václav) in St. Vitus Cathedral. This symbolically-charged chapel, dedicated to the patron saint of Bohemia, constitutes an example of high Gothic art during the reign of Charles IV, and is similar in style to the castle at Karlštejn. The chapel is a true showcase designed to house religious relics and serve as focal point for worship of the national saint.

Other churches have also retained their Gothic interiors, among them the Karlov church (Na Karlově) in New Town, founded by Charles IV. The bold vaulting in the form of an eight-pointed star was reconstructed following a fire in 1575. Further examples are the church of St. Peter on Na poříčí (one of the oldest in Prague, with a Romanesque façade and a Gothic choir dating from the fourteenth and fifteenth centuries), the church of St. Apollinarus in New Town (with simple nave and wall paintings that date from 1390), and the small fourteenth-century church of the Virgin at Slupi (noteworthy not only for its vaulted ceiling that rises from a slim cylindrical pillar, but also for its needle-like steeple).

Certain Prague houses, particularly in Old Town, have also retained their Gothic interiors. The town hall dates back to 1338 when wealthy burghers bought several private houses and converted them into the seat of local government; the third floor still looks as it did in 1470. A feature peculiar to Prague are the houses near Old Town Square which are completely baroque outside (their façades having been restored in the late 1980s) yet totally Gothic inside. The Three Kings house at 3 Celetná Street (next to Our Lady of Týn Church), where the young Franz Kafka lived, is a particularly good example. Such extraordinary combinations of architectural styles bear witness to the incessant transformations that Prague has undergone over the centuries. New Town's city hall, begun around 1367, also has a large Gothic room with two naves (now used for weddings).

Prague is a city where visitors can enjoy a glass of beer or wine in taverns or bars that have remained Gothic, at least in part. These include The Golden Pitcher (U zlaténe konvice), whose walls are older than even the Charles Bridge, The Green Frog (U zelené žáby), established in 1403, and the famous alehouse St. Thomas's (U svatého Tomáše), which dates from 1352.

Prague Castle, the former Royal Palace, houses the richest and most varied Gothic interiors. The thirteenth-century vestiges of the palace of the Přemyslid king Ottakar II, can be seen today in the arcaded corridor and the restored Bureau of Provincial Registers with its vaulted ceiling that rests on two short, massive pillars. The fourteenth-century spaces include a fine columned room built under Václav IV. Finally, magnificent examples of late Gothic architecture can be admired in the room known as the Vladislav bedchamber with its superb polychrome vaulting, the Riders' Staircase with its highly original ceiling decorated by a network of broken ribbing, and the monumental, sixty-seven-yard-long Vladislav Hall, built from 1493 to 1502. These interiors date from the reign of Vladislav Jagiello and mark the summit of flamboyant Gothic architecture before the development of a Renaissance style that was slow in reaching Bohemia.

There are few Renaissance buildings in Prague, and the art of the period constitutes what may be characterized as a transitional style between the flamboyant Gothic and the baroque. The Ludvík wing of Prague Castle, built between 1502 and 1509, is a blend of late Gothic and early Renaissance, as is the old Diet with its Renaissance gallery where the Diet clerk was seated.

Renaissance architecture is primarily evident in highly ornamented buildings such as Hvězda (Star) villa, which takes its name from the floor plan in the shape of a six-pointed star. It was decorated between 1555 and 1556 with frescoes by Italian architects commissioned by Archduke Ferdinand of Tyrol. The Belvedere, or Royal Summer Palace (Belvedér or Královské letohrádek) built for Queen Anne, was also designed by Italian artists but its original interior has largely disappeared, with the exception of the roofing in the shape of an upside-down ship's hull covered with copper plate. The Renaissance style is also reflected in the Large Hall and Small Hall of the old tennis courts. These façades are richly decorated with incised patterns known as sgraffito. Apart from the Hvězda Villa, however, such buildings (like the Spanish Hall and the Rudolf Gallery, built during the reign of Rudolf II) have lost their original interiors either due to destruction by various armies — Swedish in 1648, Franco-Bavarian in 1741–1742 and Prussian in 1757 — or to unfortunate renovations and restorations carried out during the nineteenth century.

Other Renaissance interiors have survived, however, such as the former Lobkovic Palace, now known as Schwarzenberg Palace, where the ceiling paintings date from 1580. Martinic Palace, completed around 1624, also has fine painted ceilings. The Pinkas Synagogue, rebuilt in a late Renaissance style in the early seventeenth century has been restored and its ribbed vaulting is once again visible.

Baroque architecture found one of its highest expressions in Prague and gave the city its distinctive skyline. Baroque art was ideologically associated with the Counter-Reformation, and therefore was long considered to be a style imposed from the outside. This view held that baroque art swept through Bohemia only after the Battle of the White Mountain in 1620, a defeat that simultaneously marked the end of national independence for three hundred years, the demise of the religious tolerance for which Bohemia had so staunchly struggled, and a forced return to Catholicism. In fact, baroque art appeared earlier, during the reign of Matthias, who deposed his brother Rudolf II in 1611. Moreover, the baroque style was a logical extension of the mannerist style prevalent under Rudolf II. The baroque style readily took root in Prague, where it constitutes an integral characteristic of the city, giving certain neighborhoods the "Italian" air noted by Chateaubriand during a stay in 1833. The palaces in Hradčany and Malá Strana, with their Italianate gardens, and the houses in Kampa and Old Town Square gave Prague a reputation for being the "northern Florence." This collection of baroque palaces, churches, and gardens is decorated by countless statues (saints, caryatids, angels, nymphs, mythological figures, warriors and so on) that watch over the city from on the Charles Bridge, from the façades and rooftops, or in gardens, lending Prague its fascinating, theatrical ambience.

Given the great number of baroque interiors, both palatial and ecclesiastic, only the most renowned can be mentioned here. The church of St. Nicholas (sv. Mikulás) in Malá Strana, considered to be Prague's most beautiful church, is a major feature of the Prague skyline. The church of St. John of Nepomuk on the Rock (sv. Jan Nepomucky na skalce) is one of the most original and beautiful baroque churches in Prague. St. John Nepomuk, who served as an emblem for the Counter-Reformation, was a fictional character invented by the Jesuits, based on the lives of two different people, and canonized in 1729. Another church, St. James (sv. Jakub), its façade adorned with large compositions by the Italian artist Ottavio Mosto, has a long, impressive interior with twenty-one altars and paintings by Petr Brandl and Václav Vavřinec Reiner, two of the greatest Czech baroque painters. It also houses Prague's finest baroque tombs, executed for Count Jan Václav Vratislav of Mitrovice by Ferdinand Maximilian Brokoff and designed by Fischer von Erlach. Lovers of sacred music also appreciate the church of St. James for its excellent acoustics.

Several of Prague's many baroque palaces will also be featured here as examples of secular architecture. The Wallenstein (or Valdštejn) Palace, Prague's first baroque residence, was built between 1624 and 1630 for Albrecht von Wallenstein, commander in chief of the imperial armies. It is known for the statues in the garden and large *sala terrena*. Also included are the Troja Châteleau (Trojský zámek), built between 1679 and 1685 by the Burgundian architect Jean-Baptiste Mathey, a former monastery in Zbraslav (six miles south of Prague, now a museum of Czech sculpture), the imposing Klementinum complex (which covers an area second only in size to Prague Castle), and the Clam-Gallas Palace (Clam-Gallasův palác) in Old Town, one of Prague's most beautiful baroque residences, decorated with impressive statues by Matthias Bernhard Braun, now the repository of the municipal archives.

It is also worth mentioning Lobkovic Palace (currently the German Embassy), one of Prague's most striking baroque buildings. It was built around 1705 on plans by Giovanni Battista Alliprandi. Its remarkable façade overlooks a garden and its interiors have decorative paintings that date from around 1720. Then there is Černín Palace (Černínský palác), now allocated to the Ministry of Foreign Affairs, built for Count Jan Humprecht Černín of Chudenice by Italian architect Francesco Caratti in 1669–1692 in a Palladio-inspired classical idiom. Its 150-yard-long exterior façade makes a monumental impression. Despite numerous transformations and the damage inflicted by the French and Prussian invasions in the eighteenth century, a grand staircase still survives, with frescoed ceiling painted in 1718 by Václav Vavřinec Reiner showing the fall of the Titans.

During the second half of the eighteenth century, a number of rococo interiors were added to Prague's architectural riches, mainly in Prague Castle. From 1753 to 1775, Niccolo Pacassi, architect to the court of Vienna, totally renovated the castle and the results remain today. He converted the buildings to the west of the Royal Palace into a single group organized around three courtyards, and added a uniform façade in late rococo style, as well as audience rooms in the same style inside. The best preserved rococo interiors, however, are to be found in the Archbishop's Palace (Archbiskupský palác) on Castle Square outside the castle. In addition to a baroque and rococo façade, the Archbishop's Palace houses a chapel with ceiling frescoes as well as French tapestries and collections of porcelain and paintings.

The flowering of the baroque and rococo hardly represents the last great period of architecture in Prague. The city offers some fine examples of neoclassicism such as the Estates Theater (Stavovské divadlo), built in 1781–1783. Empire architecture is represented by Masaryk Station (Masarykovo nádraží) the oldest in Prague, inaugurated in 1845, the church of the Holy Cross (built between 1816 and 1824 on Na příkopě Avenue) and the Kinský Villa (1827–1831, located in the pleasant Petřín gardens in Smíchov and home to a collection of folk costumes and art).

The third golden age of Prague architecture began in 1850 and reached its height at the turn of the century. Beginning with revival styles — neo-Gothic, neo-Renaissance, neo-baroque, neo-rococo — it developed into a regional variation of Art Nouveau known as Secession style. Some of the city's most important buildings were built during this period and form a dominant characteristic of Prague's current skyline. These include the

National Museum (Národní muzeum), the National Theater (Národní divadlo), the Municipal House (Obecní dům), and Prague's main train station (Praha hlavní nádraží) (formerly Franz Josefs Bahnhof). This period was closely linked to two historical developments — the revival of fervent nationalism, and the growth of Bohemia's economic, industrial and financial might. The joint impact of these two developments would give Prague — a city deprived of political power until 1918 — buildings that lent it the appearance of a capital city. Prague architecture in the second half of the nineteenth century reflected an ambiguous situation — Bohemia was subordinate to Vienna in political terms, yet was the wealthiest and most industrialized part of the Austro–Hungarian empire. This political subservience, combined with a need to assert national culture, led to the development of a nationalist movement that struggled to defend local language, literature and traditions, and which found architectural expression in buildings such as the National Museum and National Theater, as well as in exterior and interior decorative motifs drawn from the Czech nation's legendary origins and heroes.

Economic might was translated into architecture in the form of banks, some of which were designed as veritable monuments to the glory of Bohemian wealth. A few, like the Bank of the Lands of the Bohemian Crown, participated in the development of national culture through art patronage. The architectural expression of affluence could also be seen in concert halls and theaters such as the Rudolfinum and the Vinohrady Theater, in public buildings such as the Koruna and Lucerna Palaces with their restaurants (and, in the latter case, galleries of luxury shops, theater and ballroom), and in elegant houses on the celebrated Paris Avenue.

The building that crowns these twin trends is the Municipal House. It was both a Czech social center (at a time when Prague's social and cultural life was simultaneously Czech and German) and a cultural center (with a 1,500-seat concert hall dedicated to Smetana, the father of modern Czech music).

During the period when the Municipal House was being built, certain architects adopted a style dubbed "modernism," based on English, Dutch and American architecture. They sought to translate a building's function into straight lines and flat surfaces, replacing the ornamental density of Secession style with geometric patterns (often obtained by the use of brick). This trend endowed Prague with house interiors like the one in Vinohrady built in 1908–1909 by Jan Kotěra for the publisher Laichter. In the 1920s, Prague was the only city where an attempt was made to translate cubism into architecture, as seen in the House at the Black Madonna (Dům U černé Matky boží) in Old Town, a stone's throw from the Powder Tower and the Municipal House. It fits in well with its surroundings, which is typical of Prague, a city in which different styles manage to blend together harmoniously.

Also worth mentioning are the rondo-cubist interiors of the Bank of the Czechoslovak Legions, built in 1921–1923 by Josef Gočár, and the Adriatica Bank by Pavel Janák and Josef Zasche (1922–1925). Functionalist interiors from the 1920s and 1930s include the church of St. Wenceslas in Vršovice by Gočár (1929–1930) and the Müller Villa built by Adolf Loos in Střešovice in 1929.

As this list shows, Prague offers a wide variety of interiors, and the final choice for inclusion in this book was particularly difficult. In addition, certain buildings which are logical choices for inclusion are currently closed for restoration; this is the case for the Vrtba Palace, a late Renaissance building that possesses a magnificent baroque terraced garden designed by architect Maxmilián Kaňka and completed around 1720, with statues by Matthias Bernhard Braun, and a *sala terrena* decorated with paintings by Václav Vavřinec Reiner. This enchanting spot is often cited as a typical baroque garden. Also temporarily closed is the bar U Svatého Tomáše (St. Thomas's) in Malá Strana, one of the oldest and most famous taverns in Prague, founded in 1358. Today, the tavern building is mainly Renaissance with baroque renovations and a vaulted cellar.

Furthermore, since the "Velvet Revolution" in late 1989 and the change in government, many buildings have been returned to their former owners. Some that were previously open to the public are now closed, while others are being renovated. This is true for the Strahov monastery and library with its two famous rooms ("theology" and "philosophy"), one baroque and the other classical. Under the Communist regime, Strahov housed the Museum of National Literature; it has been returned to the Premonstrant order and is now closed for restoration. It is sometimes difficult to discover and locate the new owners of mansions and buildings that recently belonged to the state, making it impossible to obtain authorization to photograph them.

Finally, there are buildings that have undergone so many restorations and transformations in appearance and use that one hesitates to include them. Such restorations concern, for example, the Emmaus Monastery and the House at the Stone Bell (Dům U kamenného zvonu). The former is a Slavonic-rite monastery founded by Charles IV in 1347, and which was particularly appreciated by Paul Claudel when he was French consul in Prague in the early twentieth century. The cloister still has its medieval paintings, but was partially destroyed by aerial bombardment at the end of the Second World War, leading to major restoration. The House at the Stone Bell in Old Town Square dates from the fourteenth century. Gothic wall paintings still grace the interior, but the exterior has recently been somewhat exaggeratedly restored to its original appearance, which had been hidden by a neo-baroque façade in the nineteenth century.

Prague holds countless surprises, on all levels. The hidden splendors featured here reflect the scope of the city's extraordinary architectural heritage.

ROMANESQUE AND GOTHIC

To understand the important role played by Bohemia during this long period, one need only evoke the reign of Charles IV, king of Bohemia and Holy Roman Emperor.

Charles was the son of John of Luxembourg, who was offered the Bohemian crown in 1310 following the assassination of the last ruler of the Přemyslid dynasty, Václav III, in 1306. Charles of Luxembourg was raised at the court of France by the future Pope Clement VI. His rise to power began in 1341 when the assembly of Bohemian nobles selected him as their king. Through skillful diplomacy, he succeeded in obtaining the support of the Electors of Germany, who named him Holy Roman Emperor in 1346. Charles traveled to Italy in 1354, and in 1355 was elected king of Lombardy before going to Rome a few months later to be solemnly crowned emperor. Charles IV's ambitious policy of alliances progressively enlarged the hereditary lands of the Luxembourg dynasty and his Golden Bull of 1356 designated the crown of Bohemia as the principal lay Elector of the empire.

Heir to the Přemyslid dynasty through his mother and grandson of King Václav II, Charles was highly cultivated and extremely conscious of historical symbols that might reinforce the legitimacy of his reign; he therefore deliberately sought to perpetuate the tradition of his Přemyslid ancestors, who had ruled Bohemia from the ninth century to the early fourteenth century. Under the Přemyslids, Bohemia had also experienced periods of great economic and artistic wealth, notably toward the end of the dynasty, when its kings became powerful Electors of the Holy Roman Emperor.

During Charles's reign Bohemia enjoyed its golden age, becoming a major center of European culture. In 1348 Charles founded central Europe's first university in Prague, as well as a town—Nové Město—to accommodate the students and clergy. Prague remained an important intellectual center throughout the fourteenth and fifteenth centuries, as well as a theater of religious debate. Under Václav IV (1378–1419), son of Charles IV, a nationalist reaction with strong social overtones set in. This movement is named after its instigator, Jan Hus, who was rector of the university. The Hussite wars profoundly marked the period, and the violent iconoclasm of Hus's followers led to extensive damage to many buildings in Prague. The movement also foreshadowed the Protestant Reformation that would spread through Europe in the early sixteenth century.

Saint Wenceslas Chapel, Saint Vitus Cathedral (see p. 23).

Church of Saint George

T he Church of St. George (Kostel sv.
Jiří) was built in around 920 for Prince
Vratislav of the ruling Přemyslid family
and was the second place of worship at
Prague Castle. The church was
consecrated in 925 by Bishop Tuto de
Ratisbonne. The church houses the tombs
of the early Přemyslid princes, including
that of its founder. Princess Mlada, sister
of Prince Boleslav II, founded Bohemia's
first convent there, of the Benedictine
order, and became its first abbess in 973,
which was the year—not by coincidence
—that Prague was elevated to the status
of a cathedral city. As a result, the
original, rather simple church was
transformed into a basilica with three
naves, reputed to be an artistic
masterpiece of the period. In the late
eleventh century, the church was further
enlarged and the ceiling heightened. A fire
in 1142 led to major renovation work,
which resulted in the Romanesque
appearance the church has today.
Sometime after 1500 a Renaissance portal
was added to the south side of the
basilica. The addition was designed by
German mason Benedikt Ried (who also
designed the famous Vladislav Hall in the
Royal Palace). The baroque period
contributed a new western façade to the
church, probably designed by Francesco
Caratti. Between 1888 and 1918, the
basilica was largely restored to its
Romanesque appearance.

ROMANESQUE HOUSE (3 U RADNICE)

Only the original ground floor still exists of a three-storey Romanesque house, which was built during the second half of the twelfth century (left). Now below today's street level, the main space is nearly quadrangular in shape, with four ribbed vaults rising from a central column. On the south side there is a narrow room with a staircase that leads upstairs. The simple architectonic forms are clearly related to those of the Romanesque monastery at Strahov. Most of Prague's Romanesque houses were built on the current site of Old Town, during the reign of King Vladislav II (1140–1172). They constitute an ensemble unique in Europe, in particular because of the variety and complexity of their floor plans. They apparently represent a purely local phenomenon that sprang up independently of influence from other urban centers in Europe.

HOUSE OF THE LORDS OF KUNŠTÁT

Located on Řetězová Street in the center of Old Town, this Romanesque house (above) represents the pinnacle of twelfth-century secular architecture in Prague. It is a two-storey house with a grand staircase along one side. The ground floor (now below street level) has retained its original layout of a central hall divided into two naves; the six ribbed vaults of the ceiling rest on two cylindrical pillars. The two side rooms each have a central pillar and a chimney. This residence belonged to Boček of Kunštát during the first half of the fifteenth century. Kunštát was the uncle of George of Poděbrady, who was elected king of Bohemia in 1458. The house was carefully restored and converted into a Poděbrady museum in 1983.

OLD-NEW SYNAGOGUE

The Old-New Synagogue (Staronová synagóga) is the oldest existing synagogue in Europe (left). It was built between 1270 and 1275, in the transitional period between the Romanesque and the Gothic. The central part of the building is composed of an early Gothic rectangular hall with two naves; a particularly interesting feature is the five-ribbed vaulting seen in the bays separated by two octagonal pillars. The vault bosses, the capitals and the consoles at the base of the ogival ribbing are all decorated with vegetal motifs. The stone benches against the north and south walls (now covered with wood) are part of the original building. The area between the two pillars includes a bema (raised pulpit) surrounded by a wrought-iron grill decorated with both late Gothic and Renaissance motifs. The central part of the synagogue is surrounded by lower-ceilinged annexes on three sides: the vestibule to the south (the oldest area, with its archaic-looking vaults), the seventeenth-century gallery to the west, and the north gallery built in 1731–1732. (During religious services, the two galleries were reserved for women, while men worshipped in the central nave).

SAINT MARY OF THE SNOWS

When Charles IV created Prague's "New Town," there was a surge of religious and secular construction. This included the church of St. Mary of the Snows (Panna Marie Sněžná), founded by the king in 1347 near the ramparts surrounding Old Town. Charles IV bestowed the church (right) on the Carmelite convent and intended it to be the tallest religious building in Prague. But the vault of the presbytery, 110 feet high, collapsed in the sixteenth century and the church was never completed. During the Hussite period, crowds went to hear reformer Jan Želivský preach there. In 1606, the dilapidated church was given to the Franciscans, who rebuilt the vault. The interior of the church is dominated by the high altar, executed between 1649 and 1651—it is the largest altar in Prague, as well as one of the oldest examples of this style of baroque architecture.

SAINT VITUS CATHEDRAL

The Gothic cathedral of St. Vitus (katedrála svatého Víta) was founded in 1344 by the future Charles IV on the site of a tenth-century church, when Prague became an archdiocese. The construction was initially entrusted to Matthias of Arras, whom Charles summoned from Avignon; the design was thus heavily influenced by French cathedrals, particularly the cathedral at Narbonne. Matthias, who built the apses and the lower part of the choir up to the triforium, died in 1352, and in 1356 Charles named Peter Parler (Parléř) from Gmünd in Swabia to continue. Parler completed the choir, erected the Golden Gate (the south portal with its mosaic representing the Last Judgment), and began the nave. The sculptural decoration was also by Parler's workshop, including twenty-one busts carved directly into the sandstone walls of the triforium between 1375 and 1385, which depict members of the ruling Luxembourg dynasty and figures associated with the construction of the cathedral. Despite numerous attempts, the western part of the cathedral was not completed until 1926, based on neo-Gothic designs by architect Josef Mocker. St. Vitus Cathedral has played an important symbolic role in the history of Bohemia, and it is where the kings are buried and the crown jewels are kept.

SAINT WENCESLAS CHAPEL
SAINT VITUS CATHEDRAL

Built between 1362 and 1367 in St. Vitus Cathedral on the site where the national patron saint was buried, the chapel of St. Wenceslas was designed to recall a reliquary. The interior of the chapel (p. 14) is richly decorated. The walls are incrusted with semi-precious stones from Bohemia. In addition, the lower section of the walls of the chapel are covered with fourteenth-century frescoes depicting the Passion of Christ while the upper section has a cycle of paintings showing the legend of St. Wenceslas. This cycle is attributed to the Master of Litoměřice who incarnated the transition from flamboyant Gothic to Renaissance art in Bohemia in the early sixteenth century. The statue of Saint Wenceslas over the altar dates from 1373 and is attributed to Jindřich Parler (Parléř). Above the statue are portraits of King Vladislav Jagiello and Queen Anne. The door has a bronze Romanesque knocker in the form of a lion's head with a ring in its mouth; according to legend, Prince Wenceslas clung desperately to this very ring when he was being murdered by his brother's henchmen.

LATE GOTHIC
AND RENAISSANCE

Despite incessant dynastic conflicts and the upheavals of the Protestant Reformation, the late fifteenth and early sixteenth centuries were marked in Prague and throughout Bohemia by a cultural resurgence and the blossoming of urban and palatial architecture. Flamboyant Gothic, Vladislav Gothic, Renaissance, and mannerism were the major artistic tendencies of the period, which was characterized politically by the rule of two foreign dynasties: the Polish Jagiellos and the Austrian Hapsburgs. Vladislav II (1471–1516), the first Jagiello ruler, was selected as king by the Bohemian Estates following the death of George of Podebrady. In 1490 Vladislav was also elected king of Hungary and his son Louis II inherited the two crowns upon his death. When Louis was killed by the Turks during the disasterous Battle of Mohács in 1526, the Bohemian Estates' choice for the next king fell upon Ferdinand of Hapsburg, archduke of Austria and later Holy Roman Emperor, whose dynasty was granted hereditary rights to the Bohemian throne.

The main exponent of Vladislav Gothic was Benedikt Ried, who used elements of flamboyant Gothic style to develop a more modern concept of space, in line with parallel developments in Italian Renaissance architecture. Bonifac Wohlmut, who succeeded Ried as the official architect of Prague Castle, brilliantly wedded Palladian architecture to the local late Gothic style. Starting in the 1540s, a number of artists from northern Italy came to Prague to pursue their careers, thereby contributing to the spread of new artistic ideas.

The Hapsburg emperor Rudolf II (1576–1612) took up residence in Prague Castle in 1583. In the tradition of Charles IV, Rudolf made Prague the capital of the empire and the city became a major cultural center during his reign. An avid collector and a generous patron, Rudolf invited artists and scholars to his court, which by 1600 had attracted an international community of painters such as Giuseppe Arcimboldo, Hans von Aachen, Bartholomaus Spranger, and Roelant Savery, whose unique form of late Northern mannerism gave rise to the artistic movement known as the School of Prague.

Vladislav Hall, Prague Castle (see p. 26).

PRAGUE CASTLE — OLD ROYAL PALACE

The old Royal Palace (Královský palác) is located within Prague Castle (Pražský hrad), symbol of the Czech capital's thousand-year history. It was originally a pre-Romanesque fortress, the seat of the ruling Přemyslid family. The Royal Palace itself was begun in the tenth century. It has been destroyed and rebuilt so often down through the ages that its architecture reflects an enormous range of stylistic influences, from the Romanesque period to the twentieth century. Vladislav Hall (p. 24) is Prague's largest secular medieval interior, as well as being one of the finest examples of the flamboyant Gothic style in Central Europe. In 1484, King Vladislav Jagiello decided to rebuild the Royal Palace, which had been devastated and abandoned during the Hussite wars. He confided this task to Benedikt Ried (1454–1534), a key figure in late Gothic and early Renaissance architecture in central Europe. In order to build

the majestic hall (203 feet long, 38 feet wide and 43 feet high), Ried had to eliminate the entire third floor of the ceremonial wing of the palace. While the façade includes Renaissance features (for example, the tall, paired windows), the interior is a masterpiece of the flamboyant Gothic style. The extremely intricate lierne vaulting has curved ribbing that meets at the pinnacle to form five six-pointed stars, inside of which are smaller six-pointed stars. The sweeping ribs — some of which suddenly break off, ready to project into space — seem to defy gravity and lend an extraordinary impression of lightness and wave-like rhythm to the entire vault. The hall was initially used for important ceremonies, royal celebrations, and even tournaments. After the royal court was transferred to Vienna, however, Vladislav Hall was rarely used for important events. Between the sixteenth and nineteenth

century, it even served as a marketplace, the spaces between the windows were fitted with shelving on which merchants and craftsmen displayed their wares. When official ceremonies were scheduled, this shelving would be hidden behind tapestries belonging to the castle.

The chamber where the former Diet met (preceding page), endowed with a ribbed vault following the fire of 1541, was restored in 1559–1563 by imperial architect Bonifác Wohlmut. Until 1847, this hall was where the Supreme Court of the Lands of the Bohemian Crown and representatives of the Czech Estates met. The royal throne, dating from the 1830s, is in the place of honor between the windows, together with the Renaissance gallery where the chief clerk of the Kingdom of Bohemia sat.

The Bureau of Provincial Registers (p. 26) was renovated in 1486 in late Gothic style by master builder Hans Spiess. The vault is painted with the coats of arms of the higher-ranking magistrates of the aulic (or royal) tribunal who had

taken up their functions in the Bureau of Provincial Registers.

The new Hall of Provincial Registers dates from the reign of King Vladislav Jagiello (early sixteenth century). Provincial estate registers were deposited with the supreme tribunal of the Bohemian Crown. These registers recorded the rights attached to feudal property, their modifications, the tribunal's decisions and decisions made by the Estates, including conclusions of official sessions of the Estates of Bohemia. All decisions became enforceable once they were recorded in the registers, which therefore constituted the main source of civil law. This hall housed the registers of estates starting in 1541, earlier records were destroyed in the fires that ravaged Malá Strana and Prague Castle. The hall still contains a finely-worked cabinet (above) dating from 1562, the oldest of the cabinets designed to store registers. For a very short period, from 1867 to 1868, this cabinet also held the crown jewels.

HVĚZDA VILLA

This country residence, which was built in the hunting grounds of Emperor Ferdinand I in the forest of Malejov is a masterpiece of central European Renaissance architecture. The three-storey building was designed in the shape of a six-pointed star, from which it takes its name. It was built in 1555-1556 by Archduke Ferdinand of Tyrol, son of Emperor Ferdinand I and imperial governor of Bohemia, for his wife. The ground floor, with its diamond-shaped rooms arranged around a central hall, is the most impressive part of the interior. The ceilings are decorated with fine stucco work done by anonymous Italian artists and are divided into three hundred and thirty-four sections, each of which shows a scene from classical mythology.

PINKAS SYNAGOGUE

Construction on the Pinkas Synagogue (Pinkasova synagóga) began in 1535. Archaeological digs in the 1950s, however, brought to light vestiges which suggest that a Romanesque synagogue may have existed on the site in the eleventh or twelfth century. The current synagogue (left) was originally a private one, built in a residence belonging first to Israel Pinkas, then to his son-in-law Meir Horowitz, and finally to Horowitz's descendants. Initially constructed in a late Gothic style, the Pinkas Synagogue was renovated in a late Renaissance manner by architect Judas of Herz in the early seventeenth century. It was flooded several times, notably in 1771 and 1860, and underwent various modifications in the nineteenth century. A sixteenth-century rabbinical decree instructing that antiquated furnishings be carefully buried, ensured that all the original elements have survived, such as the bema (raised pulpit), the Holy Ark, and the Renaissance portal. The Pinkas Synagogue's magnificent Renaissance polychrome vault with its finely ribbed arches has now been restored.

KOLOWRAT PALACE

The Kolowrat Palace, linked in name to an old Bohemian aristocratic family whose members often held high government positions, is an early example of the first period of baroque architecture. The palace (right) is near the Estates Theater, which is why it was converted into a restaurant and café for theater-goers, with a small experimental theater upstairs. During the conversion, construction workers discovered beautiful ceilings with painted beams, in a style exemplifying the transition between Renaissance and early baroque.

THE BAROQUE

The beginning of the baroque period in Bohemia is linked to the upheavals of the Thirty Years' War. The insurrection of the Estates of Bohemia and Moravia was led by Protestant nobles in reaction to the intolerance of Emperor Matthias (1611–1620). The uprising was crushed in the Battle of the White Mountain in 1620 and the rebels were severely punished through executions, exile and confiscation of property. The outcome and repercussions of the Battle of the White Mountain determined the fate of Bohemia for decades to come.

In 1627 Ferdinand II enacted a new constitution, which instituted a systematic reorganization of the government. The Estates were forbidden any legislative role, the king was given supreme executive powers, and German was introduced as a second official language, thereby legalizing the Germanization of Bohemia. Catholicism was declared the official religion, which resulted in the persecution and massive emigration of Bohemia's Protestants. The broad range of Counter-Reformation measures enacted included the establishment in 1628 of a Jesuit province and the arrival or return of numerous other Catholic religious orders.

Despite being the fruit of a tragic situation, baroque art and architecture in Bohemia were both brilliant and original. The particularity of Bohemian baroque has often been the subject of debate, but it is clear that the baroque style rapidly became integrated and soon lost its foreign character. Bohemia became the second home of a radical school of Italian baroque art and was the birthplace of an original revival style called baroque Gothic. Many painters and sculptors, often foreign, were drawn to Bohemia. Writing about this remarkable period Antonin Matějček, the Czech art historian, pointed out, "Within the baroque world, Bohemian soil produced an original offshoot of international baroque art, endowed with remarkable vitality and wonderful fertility."

Troja Château (see p. 36).

WALLENSTEIN PALACE

An early example of the baroque architecture that would later profoundly mark Prague, the magnificent Wallenstein Palace (Valdštejn palác) was built between 1623 and 1630. The site was originally occupied by twenty-three houses and three gardens. The palace was built for Albrecht von Wallenstein, duke of Friedland and commander of the Imperial Catholic armies. The palace is also a symbol of the troubled period of the Thirty Years' War, because Wallenstein's unscrupulous confiscation of property from the rebels during the repression of the revolt of the Bohemian Estates constituted one of the main sources of his wealth.

The palace was the work of two Italian architects— Andrea Spezza and, from 1628 onward, Giovanni Battista Pieroni (who was responsible for the *sala terrena*, considered to be the finest part of the ensemble). The architecture is a combination of several mannerist styles, predominantly northern Italian along with northern European and Dutch influences. This stylistic mixture is evident in the main hall, known as the Knights' Hall (left), lit by two rows of windows. The stuccoes and frescoes are the work of Bartolomeo Baccio di Bianco, and the fresco on the ceiling shows Wallenstein himself as the god Mars riding in the chariot of victory. The other rooms of the palace are richly decorated and still have their original fireplaces (above). The *sala terrena*, where concerts are now held, in particular during the annual Prague Spring Festival, hosted Friedrich von Schiller's famous play *Wallenstein* in 1859.

Troja Château

One of the first residences built outside of Prague was the charming summer château in the former hamlet of Troja (top and bottom left). The Troja Château (Trojský zámek) adapted the basic plan of a Roman villa to the new principles of baroque classicism, and was built in 1679–1691 for Count Václav Adalbert of Šternberk and his wife, Clara of Malzan. The architect, Jean-Baptiste Mathey (Matheus Burgundus), was a key figure in the emergence of Prague baroque architecture; born in Dijon and trained in Rome, Mathey was called to Prague in 1675 by Archbishop (and Count) Wallenstein. The interior of the château is richly decorated with murals (1689–1690) by Italian artists Francesco and Giovanni Marchetti. The tempera paintings on the walls of the Imperial Hall were done between 1690 and 1697 by Antwerp artists Abraham and Isaak Godyn. These paintings depict the apotheosis of the Hapsburgs—symbolically associated with Šternberk's own family—complete with classical details and Christian motifs. The Godyns were among the first to have used trompe l'oeil techniques, which were widespread during this period, on so vast a scale.

Clam-Gallas Palace

Clam-Gallas Palace (Clam-Gallasův palác) is one of the most important baroque buildings in Prague (right). It was built in the years 1713–1729 for Count Johann Wenzel Gallas, who was viceroy of Naples (the Austrian Hapsburgs occupied the kingdom of Naples from 1713 to 1734). The palace was designed by the famous Viennese architect Johann Bernhard Fischer von Erlach, who also designed the Karlskirche in Vienna and a palace for Prince Eugène of Savoy. His style reflected a synthesis of Italian baroque influences with Mansart's French classicism. The sculptures in Clam-Gallas Palace were executed by Matthias Bernhard Braun; note especially the atlantes (the male figures supporting the portals), the reliefs depicting the adventures of Hercules, the vases and the putti. The frescoes, notably the one on the ceiling over the staircase portraying the Triumph of Apollo, are the work of Carlo Innocenzo Carlone, an Italian painter from Como.

CHURCH OF SAINT NICHOLAS IN MALÁ STRANA

The church of St. Nicholas (sv. Mikuláš) occupies the south side of the former Jesuit college and was built in the early eighteenth century. It was erected on the site of a Gothic church of the same name in Prague's Malá Strana (Little Quarter). It is an excellent example of classically-inspired baroque illusionism. The church's refined construction, based on Christoph Dientzenhofer's plan of three intersecting ovals, constituted a veritable architectonic experiment at the time. After the death of Dientzenhofer, the church was finally completed by his son Kilian Ignaz during a phase of construction that began in 1735; the choir was completed and a huge dome erected in 1751. Both interior and exterior are characterized by a wealth of forms and sense of movement. The most important high baroque artists in Prague participated in decorating the interior. The main vault is decorated with a fresco celebrating the glory of St. Nicholas, executed by Jan Lukas Kracker in 1761. The dome was painted by František Xaver Palko, who was also responsible for the frescoes above and below the gallery. Underneath the dome are four colossal statues depicting the Doctors of the Church, sculpted in 1769 by Ignác-František Platzer, who was responsible for most of the sculpture in the church, including the copper statue of St. Nicholas on the high altar.

CHURCH OF SAINT MARGARET BENEDICTINE MONASTERY IN BŘEVNOV

The oldest monks' abbey in Bohemia is the Benedictine Monastery in Břevnov. It is now one thousand years old, and was founded jointly in 993 by Bishop Vojtěch (canonized and better known by the name of St. Adalbert) and Prince Boleslav II. Archaeological digs have uncovered an early eleventh-century pre-Romanesque crypt beneath the choir. The monastery buildings were sacked and practically destroyed during the Hussite wars in the fifteenth century, and replaced between 1708 and 1745 by a set of baroque buildings of outstanding artistic quality. The church of St. Margaret (sv. Markéta), with a single nave, was built between 1710 and 1715 from plans by Christoph Dientzenhofer, and features picturesque curves based on a system of interpenetrating ovals. Attribution for the design of the church was long a subject of dispute, yet is one of the finest examples of classically-inspired baroque illusionism. The vault is decorated with frescoes executed between 1719 and 1721 by Johann Jakob Steinfels: in the choir can be seen the apotheosis of the Holy Cross, St. Margaret with saints from the Benedictine order, and the patron saints of Bohemia. The trompe l'oeil altars are adorned with paintings by Petr Brandl, one of the most important baroque painters in Bohemia.

SAINT JOHN OF NEPOMUK ON THE ROCK

St. John of Nepomuk on the Rock (sv. Jan Nepomucký na skalce) is one of Prague's finest baroque churches. It was built around 1730 on a design by Kilian Ignaz Dientzenhofer. Inside the church, high walls arch up toward the vaulting, while pendentives descend very low. The ceiling (above) has a fresco of the apotheosis of St. John of Nepomuk, painted in 1748 by Jan Karel Kovář. Kovář's work is striking in its use of clear, luminous color. The church's original rococo interior has remained largely unchanged. On the high altar is a wooden model of the statue of St. John of Nepomuk on the Charles Bridge, which was executed by Jean Brokoff in 1683 from a design by Viennese sculptor Mathias Rauchmiller; this statue has inspired hundreds of nearly identical copies.

VILLA AMERIKA — ANTONÍN DVOŘÁK MUSEUM

Originally a vacation residence built for Count Jan Václav Michna of Vacínov prior to 1720, this is one of the most delightful examples of secular baroque architecture in Prague (right). It was designed by architect Kilian Ignaz Dientzenhofer, son of architect Christoph Dientzenhofer who emigrated to Prague from Germany with his five brothers. The Dientzenhofer name is linked to some of the most important baroque buildings in Prague, such as the church of St. Nicholas in Malá Strana. Kilian Ignaz built this small house on his return from Vienna, and it reveals the influence of the grand residences of the Austrian capital by architect Lucas Hildebrandt. The main hall, with a ceiling painting that depicts Apollo, was decorated by Johann-Ferdinand Schor, a painter from Innsbruck. In 1932, the Association of Friends of Antonín Dvořák transformed the villa into a museum devoted to the great composer.

Former Monastery In Zbraslav

Founded in 1292 by King Václav II, the former Cistercian monastery in Zbraslav played a key role in Bohemian history. Its founder intended it to become the burial site of the Přemyslid dynasty, in imitation of the French royal abbey of St. Denis. But the original edifice was destroyed in 1420 during the Hussite wars. It was only in the eighteenth century, between 1709 and 1739, that the Cistercian order rebuilt an impressive monastery in the form of a château.

The architects, Giovanni Santini-Aichel and František Maxmilián Kaňka, are remembered for the particular revival style they developed known as "baroque Gothic."

The château's Royal Hall on the second floor was completed in 1727 and richly decorated in stucco by Italian artists Tomaso and Martino Soldati from Lugano. The frescoes were painted in 1728 by Prague artist Václav Vavřinec Reiner; the ceiling paintings show the church foundations being consecrated, while those on the walls depict the dubbing of knights during the founding of the church and King Václav II making donations to the monastery.

Today, most of the monastery houses the National Gallery's collection of Czech sculpture from the nineteenth and twentieth centuries.

KLEMENTINUM

The Klementinum was the first college established by the
Jesuits in Bohemia. This vast complex (second only to
Prague Castle in area), with its stern, fortress-like appearance,
was systematically enlarged over many decades until the
Jesuits were expelled in 1773. The complex was organized
around five courtyards and included secular buildings such as
primary and secondary schools, libraries, a theater, an

observatory and a print shop. Major architects associated with
the birth and flowering of Prague's baroque movement
participated in the various phases of construction, such as
Carlo Lurago, Francesco Caratti, Giovanni Domenico Orsi
and František Maxmilián Kaňka. Kaňka was responsible in
1724 for the final version of the former "Chapel of Mirrors"
(right), commissioned by the Marian congregation. The

luxurious interior is richly decorated with stucco-framed mirrors and ceilings painted with episodes from the life of the Virgin Mary by Johann Hiebel, a disciple of Andrea Pozzo and brilliant student of Pozzo's trompe l'oeil fresco technique. On the walls are four paintings of saints by one of Bohemia's most important baroque painters, Václav Vavřinec Reiner. The chapel was deconsecrated in 1784 and is now used as exhibition space and as a concert hall. Another of Kaňka's masterful contributions to the Klementinum is the main room of the library (left), built between 1722 and 1727. It includes a circular gallery and trompe l'oeil frescoes by Johann Hiebel symbolizing the Arts and Sciences, while the illusionist painting in the cupola depicts the Temple of Wisdom. The Klementinum currently houses the National Library.

THUN PALACE
BRITISH EMBASSY

The Thun Palace (Thunovský palác) complex grew around the Renaissance-style residence of the counts of Leslie, dating from the first half of the seventeenth century. In 1656, the archbishop of Salzburg, Quidobald Thun-Hohenstein, bought the building, probably because it was located on the same hill as Prague Castle and dominated the surrounding landscape, thereby satisfying the vanity of one of the empire's most powerful clerics. A major baroque renovation took place between 1716 and 1727, commissioned by Osvald Thun and probably based on designs by Giovanni Battista Alliprandi.

BUQUOY PALACE—FRENCH EMBASSY

Located in a picturesque corner of Malá Strana, the French Embassy is not far from the charming island of Kampa. The palace assumed its present form shortly after 1735, when Maria Anna of Hrzán combined three of her residences: the former Waldstein palace—which had been renovated after 1719 by Countess Marie-Josephine of Thun (née Waldstein) —the former college of the Order of Malta, and a building called "the little Waldstein house." The name of the architect who carried out this operation remains unknown, but it is thought that the 1719 renovation and the work done after

1735 were based on designs by Maxmilián Kaňka, successor
to Giovanni Santini-Aichel. In 1748, the palace became the
property of Count François Léopold Buquoy. The palace
interior was largely renovated during the second half
of the nineteenth century. The main hall of the earlier

wing, which dates from 1736, is sumptuously decorated
with magnificent tapestries from the sixteenth, seventeenth
and eighteenth centuries.

At the Golden Goose—Sternegg Palace

The house known as "At the Golden Goose" is one of the finest in Malá Strana, and its façade was designed by a follower of architect František Maxmilián Kaňka. Originally a bourgeois residence, it was renovated in the seventeenth century by the Thun family, and again in the mid-eighteenth century for Leopold Gunther von Sternegg.

The richly decorated interior dates from the 1740s and is partly the work of Johann Peter Molitor (1702–1756), a painter from Koblenz in the Rhineland. His beautifully executed frescoes reflect a profound appreciation of a realistic painterly idiom.

CLASSICISM
AND REVIVAL STYLES

At the end of the eighteenth century, Prague appeared to have lost much of the artistic vitality it had shown in the preceding period, projecting, instead, the image of a quiet, sleepy provincial town. In cultural spheres, shedding this image became a challenge.

The reforms introduced by Emperor Joseph II between 1780 and 1790 — the Edict of Tolerance, the abolition of serfdom and certain financial measures — were impregnated with the progressive ideas of the Age of Enlightenment. They also, however, led to greater centralization of power and a rigid bureaucratic system. Opposition to these developments gradually hardened into a new nationalistic movement, which was supported by the aristocracy and the intelligentsia. In 1791 an industrial exposition was organized in Prague, the first such exposition on mainland Europe. It was also at this time that the first artistic and scientific societies were founded. These included the Society of Patriotic Friends of the Fine Arts, in 1796, out of which grew the Alte Pinakothek, and, in 1800, the Academy of Fine Arts.

The Napoleonic wars, the growing importance of the middle classes, and the activities of the intelligentsia gave rise to a Czech national revival. The impact of this movement was felt, initially, in the realm of language and literature, in a nation where the German-Czech bilingual culture had long been a continual source of conflict, but also one of enrichment, contributing to the development of a cosmopolitan milieu in Prague.

In 1848, following the events of the so-called Spring of Nations, the national revival assumed a political dimension. Moderates advocated the federalization of Austria, but the Austro-Hungarian Compromise of 1867 relegated the Czechs to a subordinate role.

Political events were echoed by cultural ones. Buildings were seen as expressions of economic and cultural might, and banks, museums, and theaters became, in this revivalist period, the bearers of a specific national iconography, that formed the basis for a number of artistic currents during the twentieth century. In 1891, an exposition marking the jubilee of the kingdom of Bohemia comprised one hundred and forty buildings. The exposition testified to the industrial might of Bohemia and, on an artistic level, revealed the first signs of a new style.

Foyer, National Theater (see p. 63).

Estates Theater

Built in 1781–1783, the Estates Theater (Stavovské divadlo) was financed by Franz Anton Nostitz-Rhienek, Prague's "high burgrave." The architect, Anton Haffenecker, designed it in a classical style with several dynamic baroque elements that strongly underscore local architectural tradition. The interior decoration is by two well-known artists who symbolize two different periods in Bohemia's artistic history—Jan Quirin Jahn, the last president of Prague's painters' guild, and Josef Bergler, the first director of the new Academy of Fine Arts, founded in 1799. Bergler painted the main curtain in 1804, a copy of which can be seen on the wall. The theater opened in 1783 with a performance of *Emilia Galotti*, by the famous German playwright G. E. Lessing. The theater's second director, Pasquale Bondini, produced Italian operas. After the great success of *The Marriage of Figaro* in 1786, Bondini invited Mozart and his librettist, Lorenzo da Ponte, to Prague to compose a new opera. This turned out to be *Don Giovanni*, which premiered at the Estates Theater in 1787, conducted by Mozart himself. Between 1813 and 1816, Carl Maria von Weber was the theater's musical director, and in 1828 the great violinist Niccolo Paganini gave a concert here.

FORMER VÁVRA HOUSE—POST OFFICE MUSEUM

The interior of the Vávra House (Vávrův dům) evokes the peaceful atmosphere that reigned in petit bourgeois Prague during the first half of the nineteenth century (above). It was decorated by Josef Navrátil (1798–1865), who shared his contemporaries' taste for historical and mythological scenes inspired by the world of theater, and for Romantic landscapes as beautiful as they were idealized. For his 1847 decoration of Vávra House, Navrátil used a special medium of oil-based paint on a resin ground. In the dining room, also called "the Alpine room," there are recognizable images of Altdorf on Lake Lucerne in Switzerland, as well as the Adršpach Falls in Bohemia. The paintings are complemented by their neo-rococo painted frames. Vavra House was recently restored and has been the site of the Post Office Museum (Muzeum postovní známky) since 1988.

SPANISH SYNAGOGUE

In the early sixteenth century, a group of Spanish Jews fleeing the Inquisition founded a synagogue on this site, the origin of the name Spanish Synagogue. The synagogue building was destroyed by fire and had to be rebuilt several times.

The current synagogue (right), also called the Temple, was built in the 1860s by architects Ignác Ullman and Josef Niklas. Its composite style combines pseudo-Moorish influences and European Renaissance details. The interior is richly decorated with a profusion of stucco and gilding, in imitation of the Alhambra in Grenada, Spain.

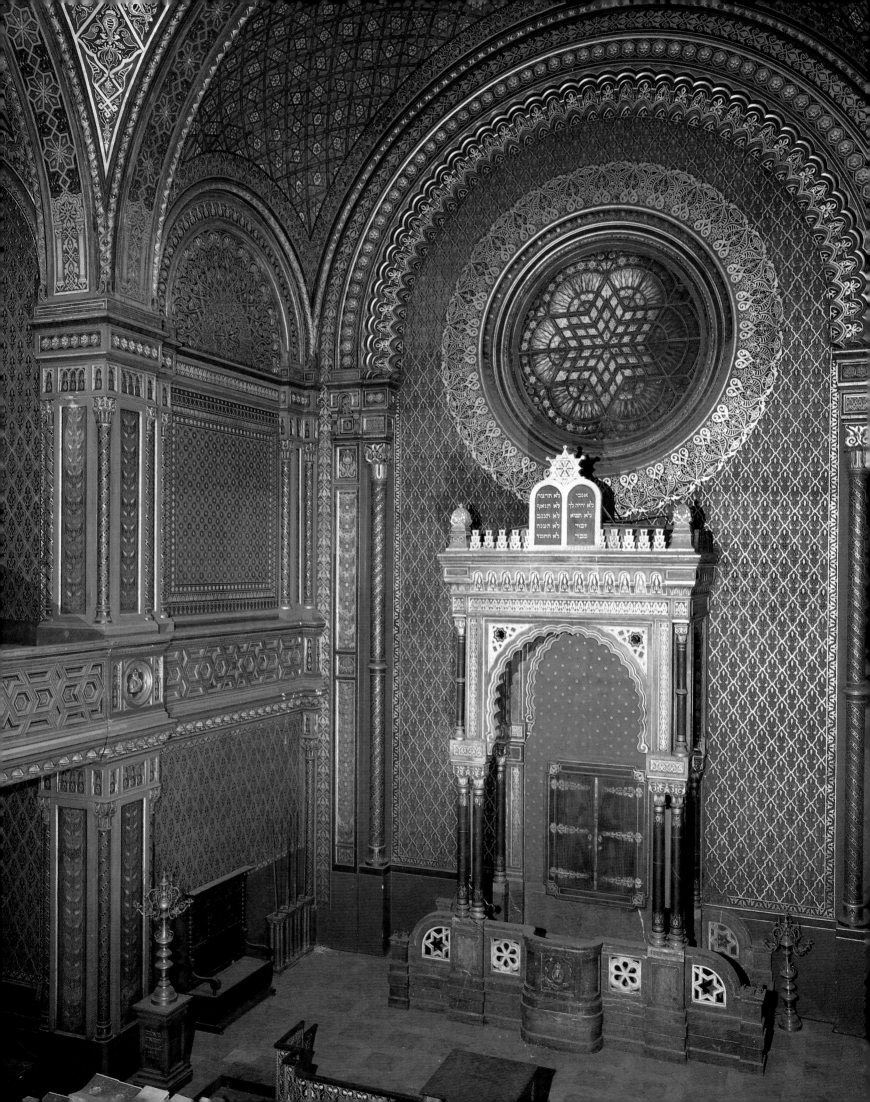

NATIONAL THEATER

The building of the National Theater (Národní divadlo) can be seen as the culmination of the process of "national revival" that fueled Czech nationalism from the late eighteenth century to the end of the nineteenth century.

The cornerstone was laid in 1868. A subscription to raise funds met with great enthusiasm throughout the country, and the theater was inaugurated on 11 June 1881, only to be partly destroyed by a fire two months later. It was rebuilt and reopened its doors on 18 November 1883, with a performance of *Libuše*, a symbolic opera by Smetana, the father of modern Czech music. Architect Josef Zítek chose a neo-Renaissance style for this monument to national culture. The interior decoration was the work of young artists barely out of art school, such as Mikoláš Aleš and František Ženíšek, who in 1878 painted the most impressive part of the theater, the foyer (p. 56). The cycle depicted in the lunettes is titled *The Fatherland*. It traces the symbolic pilgrimage of a young man across mythical and legendary sites in Bohemia's history, and prefigures the symbolist cycles that became a feature of Czech art at the turn of the century. The lunettes along the second floor corridor, by Adolf Liebscher, represent allegories of Opera, Ballet, Comedy and Tragedy. In the auditorium itself, the decorative curtain is a homage to the sacrifices made by the Czech nation in constructing the theater and was painted by Vojtěch Hynais, a disciple of the French painters Jean-Léon Gérôme and Paul Baudry.

The importance of the National Theater is the reason why all the artists who participated in its realization were later known collectively as "the National Theater generation," even if their individual artistic conceptions differed.

NATIONAL MUSEUM

Like the National Theater, the National Museum (Národní muzeum) is an edifice with symbolic significance, having been erected "for the glory of the Czech nation." The idea of founding a national museum was an old one that finally came to fruition in 1818 through the efforts of a group of patriotic nobles and intellectuals that included "the father of the nation," historian František Palacký (1796–1876). But the museum remained without a permanent home for a long time; it wasn't until 1864 that the Assembly of the Lands of the Kingdom of Bohemia decided to erect a building to host the museum's collections and activities. Another twenty years slipped by before a public competition chose Josef Schulz's sumptuous neo-Renaissance design, which was built between 1885 and 1890.

The interior of the museum is dominated by a monumental, six-branched staircase (right) with arcaded corridors lit from above. A major feature of the building is the two-storey high Pantheon dedicated to the memory of leading figures in the nation's history. On the staircase are statues of the kings of Bohemia, originally executed by Munich sculptor Ludwig Schwanthaler for an earlier Czecho-Slav pantheon to have been located outside of Prague, but which was never built. Under the glass roof are sixteen busts of museum founders, and medallions showing thirty-six kings of Bohemia by sculptor Antonín Popp. The walls of the staircase are decorated with ten paintings of Bohemian castles, executed by landscape painter Julius Mařák and his students at the Academy of Fine Arts. The Pantheon also contains statues and busts by, among others, Josef Václav Myslbek, Bohuslav Schnirch, Stanislav Sucharda, and Ladislav Šaloun. There are painted scenes depicting episodes from Bohemian history by František Ženíšek and Václav Brožík, as well as allegories of Science, Progress, Art and Inspiration by Vojtěch Hynais. These artists are members of the so-called "National Theater generation." Here, however, their work is accompanied by contributions from their students and followers associated with the Czech Secession art movement.

RUDOLFINUM

Prague's economic and cultural expansion in the 1860s made it indispensable to build a concert hall and fine arts gallery worthy of the capital of Bohemia. In 1872, the Bohemia Savings Bank decided to finance the plan.

The design competition was won by architects Josef Zítek and Josef Schulz, whose proposal united the two functions of art gallery and concert venue. The magnificent neo-Renaissance building, completed in 1884, includes several different halls. The 1,200-seat concert hall had excellent acoustics and was considered one of the finest examples of nineteenth-century Czech interior architecture. It was later named Dvořák Hall. The exhibition gallery, lit from above, hosted the annual salons held by the Fine Arts Union. Yet another area housed the collections of the Patriotic Society of Friends of Art (the

basis of the National Gallery's current collection), along with the collection of the Museum of Decorative Arts (until 1900). The building was named the Rudolfinum in honor of Archduke Rudolf, heir to the Hapsburg throne, but the name also honored Emperor Rudolf II, a great patron of the arts. The architects managed to marry revival aesthetics to the demands of modern functions. According to another major architect, Pavel Jának, the Rudolfinum was "an intersection of ideas, some of which would be encountered for the first time, others for the last time." Since its construction, the building has served various purposes (including that of national parliament, between 1918 and 1938). After substantial renovation, it is now once again a concert hall and exhibition space.

STATE OPERA — FORMER SMETANA THEATER

The State Opera (Státní opera) is a reminder of the cultural importance of the German community in Prague before the Second World War. Originally called the New German Theater, the State Opera (above) was erected on the site of a wooden predecessor in record time, between 1886 and 1888, just a few years after the completion of the Czech National Theater. It was designed by the famous team of Viennese architects, Ferdinand Fellner and Hermann Helmer, who built theaters all across Europe (Vienna, Berlin, Zurich, Fiume, Hamburg, Odessa, etc.). The opera house is a good example of the neo-Renaissance style typical of the period, with neo-rococo paintings by Eduard Veith. A focal point of German culture in Prague, it was famous for its performances of operas by Richard Wagner, and for having employed Richard Strauss as conductor.

CZECH SAVINGS BANK

The Czech Savings Bank (Česká spořitelna), formerly known as the Municipal Savings Bank, was the first public building in Prague to be constructed entirely by local craftsmen using exclusively Czech material. It was built between 1892 and 1894 and designed by architects Antonín Wiehl and Osvald Polívka, in a neo-Renaissance revival style. The original building, rectangular in plan, was three storeys high. The main hall (opposite), lit by skylights, evokes the noble lines of Palladian Renaissance architecture. The interior is decorated by well-known artists of the day, such as the famous stucco-worker Celda Klouček and painters František Ženíšek, Karel Vítězslav Mašek, Jaroslav Věšín and Mikoláš Aleš. Wiehl was known as the father of Czech neo-Renaissance architecture, but his design for the Savings Bank displays a more classical approach, so that the local style is most visible in the decorative imagery.

U Koruny Pharmacy

This pharmacy (left) is evocative not only of the nineteenth century (the period of its revival-style interior), but also of the entire history of the site it occupies. It was here in the Middle Ages, on a small square next to Old Town Square, that a colony of French merchants (called "Romans" in contemporary chronicles) began trading. The area later became a fruit market, and Prague's first pharmacies were established there, including At the Angel, founded in 1374 by the famous botanist Angelo of Florence, who lived at the court of Charles IV. Until 1887, a pharmacy existed in a house known as At the Golden Crown, the license for which was acquired in 1889 and transferred to the current U Koruny house (At the Crown). The owner thereupon restored this Gothic residence in a neo-baroque style, which explains its current appearance.

Bank of Commerce and Tradesmen

Originally known as the Bank of the Lands of the Bohemian Crown, the Bank of Commerce and Tradesmen (Živnostenská Banka) was erected in 1894–1896 by Osvald Polívka. The bank, which symbolized Czech industrial might at the time, is a masterpiece of neo-Renaissance architecture, although both exterior and interior display features of the emerging Czech Secession style.

The torch-bearing, revival-style statues on the main staircase (above) are by Bohuslav Schnirch, while the staircase leading to the third floor is decorated with frescoes by painters Karel Vítězslav Mašek and Karel Klusáček (p. 73). The allegorical sculptures just below the ceiling of the main hall (p. 72), representing the various regions of Bohemia, are the work of Stanislav Sucharda, among others. They are characterized by a naturalism almost reminiscent of folk art.

ART NOUVEAU
AND THE BEGINNINGS
OF MODERNISM

The dawn of the twentieth century brought significant changes in the political situation. The passive opposition that characterized the years following the Austro-Hungarian Compromise of 1867 slowly gave way to more active political involvement on the part of the liberal Young Czechs. National issues intensified as conflicts of interest between Czechs, whose economic and cultural importance could no longer be dismissed, and Germans, who were supported by the Austrians and pro-empire factions, sometimes led to serious clashes.

Czech political life became more diversified, giving rise to a range of parties and groups with capitalist, democratic, nationalist, social-democratic or even anarchist leanings. The progressive democratization of the Austro-Hungarian Empire led to the introduction of universal suffrage in 1907.

Cultural life was marked by this intense political activity, becoming increasingly open to international trends. A new generation of artists and intellectuals felt that developing a modern idea of the nation was as important as defining the needs of contemporary art. New concepts of architecture, the decorative arts, and painting were expressed by the Art Nouveau, modernist, symbolist, and decadent artistic movements. Debate also raged over such ideas as "the total artwork" (*Gesamtkunstwerk*) and the social role of art.

Thus the *Modern Review* was founded in 1894 as a platform for decadent art. In 1895 the *Manifesto of Czech Modernism* was published and in 1896 the first issue of *Free Tendancies* was published by the Secessionist Mánes association of artists. In 1898 the association began to develop a policy of major exhibitions, beginning with a presentation of Rodin's sculpture in 1902. During this period, a taste for French art and literature served as an important intellectual catalyst.

In 1907, The Eight, a group of young avant-garde artists associated with expressionism, made its first public appearance. In 1911 certain members of the Mánes Art Association left in order to found the cubist-inspired Group of Fine Artists. Czech cubism became renowned for its original application of cubist principles to architecture and the applied arts, going beyond a simple avant-garde movement to achieve the status — in the eyes of its practitioners — of a veritable philosophy.

Municipal House (see p. 85).

MAIN TRAIN STATION

Prague's main train station (hlavní nádraží) was
originally called the Franz Josefs Bahnhof in
honor of Emperor Franz Joseph, and is one of Europe's
handsomest stations. It symbolizes Prague's
transformation into a "modern metropolis," and was
constructed between 1900 and 1909. It was designed
by architect Josef Fanta, who employed various motifs
and techniques. The decoration combines figurative,
floral and geometric elements, while the materials
include stucco, brick, glass and metal. The central hall,
framed outside by two massive pylons themselves
crowned by cupolas, offers a remarkable wealth of

images, as do the wings reserved for offices and administration. This iconography includes historical scenes, emblems, allegories, and landscapes, not to mention figures drawn from folklore and mythology (both classical and Christian). The plethora of details complements yet contrasts with the structural rigor of the twin naves of steel and glass housing the platforms. The salon and waiting room reserved for royal (later presidential) travelers boasts an interior that is typical of Czech Secession art, in which every detail has a specific meaning, including the panoramic historical revival-style paintings, probably by Václav Jansa.

HOTEL EVROPA

The Hotel Evropa is a masterpiece of Czech Secession (or Art Nouveau) architecture. It is composed of two adjoining hotels in identical style — the Hotel Archduke Stefan designed by Bedřich Bendelmayer, and the Hotel Garni designed by Alois Dryák. Both Bendelmayer and Dryák were disciples of architect Friedrich Ohmann, a leading figure of neo-baroque architecture and a forerunner of the Secession movement.

78

The hotel constitutes one of the finest examples of naturalism in architecture, as expressed, for instance, in the decorative use of floral motifs. On the façade, wood is used in conjunction with ceramic vegetal motifs and rich wrought-iron work, giving it an almost folk art impact. The entire interior, from the main hall to the café with its series of galleries, is a mixture of wood and bronze. The remarkable stylistic unity of the interior extends to the tiniest detail.

CZECH NATIONAL INSURANCE BANK

B uilt between 1907 and 1909, the Czech National
Insurance Bank (Česká státní poyišťovna) was designed
by Osvald Polívka, one of the most respected architects of
commercial buildings. After a period marked by late
revivalism, Polívka was able to skillfully incorporate elements
from the Secession school into his work, often decorating his
façades with bright colors. The interior of the bank (left)
includes certain neoclassic and neo-Renaissance features,
styles which remained major sources of inspiration for
Polívka, along with motifs typical of the Secession
movement.

BANK OF COMMERCE

T he Bank of Commerce (Komerční banka) was constructed
between 1906 and 1908 on Na příkopě, an avenue known
for its luxury stores and banks. The building (above) was
immediately hailed by Prague modernists, even though it was
designed by Josef Zasche, who was not a member of the
modernist circle generally associated with architect Jan Kotěra
nor a disciple of Viennese architect Otto Wagner. In 1908,
the modernist review *Volné Směry* described the bank as: "A
building that is noble in its sobriety, magnificent in its
proportions." The revival-style statues by Franz Metzner, the
only figurative element, became a typical feature of Prague
architectural decoration.

JUBILEE SYNAGOGUE

The large Jubilee Synagogue (Jubilejní synagóga), built in 1905–1906, received its name in 1908 on the 60th anniversary of Emperor Franz Joseph's reign. The building is interesting for its synthesis of Art Nouveau principles with a Moorish revival style, and was designed by architects Wilhelm Stiastny and Alois Richter.

LUCERNA PALACE

Shopping arcades helped shape the urban environment of contemporary Prague. The first such arcade (above) was a passage through the Lucerna Palace (palác Lucerna), linking Vodičkova Street to Štěpánská Street, just off Wenceslas Square. Lucerna Palace is a vast complex of reception rooms, meeting places, stores, offices and apartments. It was built in two stages between 1907 and 1919 by Václav Havel, grandfather of the current president of the Czech Republic. It underwent renovation in the 1920s and 1940s.

The name Lucerna (Lantern) comes from the façade overlooking Vodičkova Street, which makes extensive use of glass; this idea is echoed in a symbolic lantern placed over the entry on Štěpánská Street.

The multi-purpose complex represents the culmination of a transformation that began during the final decades of the

nineteenth century, when Prague finally escaped its provincial image in order to become a truly modern metropolis. The arcade, with its marble-sheathed concrete structure and Moorish-style moldings was a veritable shopping mall that also offered a whole range of attractions, hence the name "bazaar" that figured on site plans. The surviving attractions include a theater, the Rokoko, and the foyer of Prague's oldest permanent movie theater, also called the Lucerna.

Arcades like Lucerna Palace were worlds unto themselves, microcosms of the middle-class society that vanished after 1948. They nevertheless retain a special, nostalgic charm and even inspired a 1974 novel by Czech writer Karel Pecka, whose protagonist entered one of these arcades by chance and ended up living there permanently, completely separated from the rest of the world.

MUNICIPAL HOUSE

Toward the end of the nineteenth century, the economic expansion and growing affluence of many cities in Bohemia, notably Prague, led to the appearance of a new type of multi-purpose building destined to become the center of social and cultural life by providing a venue for associations, lectures, exhibitions, shows, balls and other public events. Prague's grandiose Municipal House (Obecní dům) is the most accomplished example of this trend. It was built at the initiative of the Prague Citizens' Association, and the Town Council commissioned the design from architects Antonín Balšánek and Osvald Polívka.

The monumental edifice was built between 1905 and 1912 in a style that defies definition. Modern-spirited contemporaries criticized the building for its amalgam of various neo-Renaissance, neo-baroque and Secession features. Yet despite the lack of stylistic unity—both inside and out—the diversity of Municipal House provides visitors with a display of refined monumental features and stylistically sophisticated details. The restaurant (above) is decorated with an allegory of Prague painted by Artuš Scheiner.

In this formerly bilingual city, the Municipal House was a focal point for Czech culture, as underscored by the imagery used in the decoration of the interior. Many well-known Czech artists had a hand in it. The 1,500-seat Smetana Concert Hall (for a long time Prague's largest), for example, is decorated with allegorical paintings by Karel Špillar and sculptures by Ladislav Šaloun that symbolize the two most famous works of composer Smetana, the symphonic poem *My Country* and the *Czech Dances*. The salons upstairs (left) feature frescoes by Alfons Mucha, Jan Preisler, Maxmilián Švabinský, and František Ženíšek.

ALFONS MUCHA'S HOUSE

Built in 1414 for canon Václav of Radeč and later subject to baroque renovation, this residence has assumed an air of timelessness now that it is associated with painter Alfons Mucha (1860–1939), the Art Nouveau master. The interior still contains objects placed there by the artist and draftsman on his return to Bohemia after having lived in Paris (1887–1904) and the United States (1904–1910). A sort of Ali Baba's cave of Mucha's drawings and other objects typical of the period (sculpture, furniture, photographs), the interior was left untouched by his son, writer Jiří Mucha, who became the guardian of this sanctuary to his father's memory, living in the house until his own death in 1991. The house contains certain objects seen in photographs of Mucha's studio on Rue du Val-de-Grâce in Paris; these gifts, so evocative of an entire era, include the harmonium presented

to Mucha by Gauguin and the statues offered by Rodin. This amazing house is a reminder that Mucha was one of the leading lights of Art Nouveau in turn-of-the-century Paris. Mucha's reputation rested on his posters for actress Sarah Bernhardt, his lithe flower-women that graced calendars and decorative panels, his jewelry, and his decoration of the Bosnia-Herzegovina pavilion for the Universal Exposition of 1900 which was held in Paris.

Mucha's style was characterized by flowing, feminine figures that were both sensual and aloof, by floral arabesques and by traditional decorative motifs drawn from Moravian folk art, not to mention themes inspired by secret societies of Freemasonry and Rosicrucianism. This master of decorative art also designed the first stamps and banknotes for the fledgling Czechoslovak Republic.

House and Studio of Sculptor Stanislav Sucharda

The family residence and studio of sculptor Stanislav Sucharda (Suchardův dům) was built between 1905 and 1907 and designed by Jan Kotěra, who promoted a modernist Czech architecture based on functionalist principles. This house, one of the last examples of Kotěra's first creative period (characterized by floral modernism), is already nearly devoid of ornamentation, revealing the influence of English "cottage" modernism as practiced by Charles Francis Annesley Voysey and Charles Rennie Mackintosh. Kotěra, however, adapted this influence to local

traditions. The floor plan of the residential section is L-shaped, centering on a living space with a staircase, while the bedrooms are arranged around the garden. The design of both interior and exterior displays remarkable stylistic unity. The house contains several works by Sucharda, a major

Czech Secession sculptor who executed the grandiose monument to historian František Palacký on Palacký Square in Prague.

House of Publisher Jan Laichter

This masterpiece of geometric modernism was constructed in 1908–1909 and designed by the architect Jan Kotěra for the publisher Jan Laichter, who, among other accomplishments, published the writings of architects Otto Wagner and Baillie Scott.

In contrast to the smooth, finely ornamented floral façades of his earlier period, Kotěra here allows the brick structure to remain exposed, following in the wake of Dutch architect Hendrik Petrus Berlage and American architect Frank Lloyd Wright. The decorative asceticism of the arrangement of vertical and horizontal lines also extends to the functionalist interior, which combines the requirements of a publishing house with those of a residence. Interior decoration is limited to the natural beauty of the materials used (such as wood) and to geometric ornamentation, eschewing allegorical elements. Painter František Kysela also contributed to the decoration of the interior.

FRANTIŠEK BÍLEK MUSEUM

Masterpieces of symbolist architecture, the house and studio belonging to sculptor František Bílek were designed by the artist himself in 1910–1911. The pillars of the gateway in front of the house echo those found in ancient Egyptian temples and symbolize, according to Bílek, "a field of wheat . . . that supplies brothers with their daily food." Bílek also designed the building next to the main residence, which includes an unusual hall with a pillar in the form of a tree. The artist claimed that the main house symbolized summer, while the side house represented autumn. Similarly, every detail in the interior carries a symbolic meaning. The buildings house Bílek's sculptures and now belong to Prague's municipal gallery, which has transformed them into a museum dedicated to the work of this great symbolist artist.

FORMER FESTIVAL CLUB—ADRIA HOTEL

The basement of the last baroque edifice to be built on Wenceslas Square (by architect Josef Zika, prior to 1789) has an interior that will be a revelation to lovers of Secession art. This 1912 bar-club was designed by architect Matěj Blecha, an advocate of modern floral (and later, geometric) architecture. That same year, Blecha also designed the cubist Diamond house on Spálená Street. The sculptures illustrate the theme of Orpheus in the underworld, and lend the basement a fantastic atmosphere. The somewhat disturbing yet droll effect is typical of the fin de siècle mentality and the Secession style.

PRELATE'S HOUSE—MONASTERY OF ZBRASLAV

The prelate's house (above) is a remarkable part of the former Cistercian monastery at Zbraslav. It is the product of the reconstruction of a Gothic building by architect František Maxmilián Kaňka prior to 1739. After Cyril Bartoň of Dobenín bought the estate in 1910, certain parts of the prelate's house were renovated by architect Dušan Jurkovič (1910–1912). Jurkovič is considered to be a major turn-of-the-century architect, noteworthy for having introduced elements of folk architecture into his work. In this instance, he came up with ideas that were both constructive and poetic, as seen in his use of pebbles from the Berounka River (which joins the Vltava not far from Zbraslav) to decorate and underscore the vaulting.

NA LIBUŠINCE HOUSE

In the early twentieth century, Prague was a major European center of avant-garde art. A unique feature of art and architecture in Prague during this period was the application of cubism to architecture and the applied arts. This approach produced a certain number of surprising results that can still be seen in Prague, principally the work of architects Josef Gočár and Pavel Janák. One recently rediscovered architect is Emil Králíček, who designed the Na Libušince House (right) sometime after 1912. Králíček was one of the first Prague artists to use cubist forms and, starting in 1912, his work was characterized by a symbiosis of cubist with neoclassic elements, as exemplified by this residence.

THE 1920s AND 1930s

The end of the First World War spelled the collapse of the Austro-Hungarian Empire and the founding of the Czechoslovak Republic. The new nation's first president, Tomáš Garrigue Masaryk, was a well-known sociologist who led the country into independence and contracted a major alliance with France. To reinforce the stability of central European and Balkan borders, the Czechoslovak Republic signed La Petite Entente with Yugoslavia and Romania.

Czechoslovakia was a democratic country counted among the wealthier nations, but its existence was too brief to allow it to withstand the economic and political crises that soon shook Europe.

Czech art during this period was the reflection of a democratic society enjoying freedom of expression. It was the fruit of a modern culture that accepted and cultivated avant-garde concepts, while remaining open to more traditional approaches. Prague was a city where many functionalist buildings were constructed alongside neo-classical edifices. Cubism, poeticism, civilism, artificialism, abstract art and surrealism all found expression in the various artistic groups and movements of the day. The key role played by international exchanges at the time could be seen in the international expositions held in Prague and elsewhere in Europe as well as the United States—in particular the Exposition Internationale des Arts Décoratifs held in Paris in 1925.

By the late 1930s, however, Czechoslovakia's political situation became extremely difficult. The Prague government had to cope with national minorities—notably German and Slovak—and the 1938 Munich agreement deprived the country of the Sudetenland, opening the way for the German invasion of March 1939 which precipitated the Second World War.

Villa Traub (see p. 105).

BANK OF THE CZECHOSLOVAK LEGIONS

The Bank of the Czechoslovak Legions (Banka Československých Legií), now the Czech Bank of Commerce, was built between 1921 and 1923. It is one of the most original as well as one of the most controversial examples of modern Czech architecture. It was designed by Josef Gočár, one of the main partisans of cubism in architecture and the applied arts, who was also a founder and champion of the Czech "national style" known as rondo-cubism. This style emerged during and after the First World War, and was characterized by decorative arcs, circles and rectangles often associated with the color combinations of white and red or red and yellow, which were an allusion to Czech folk art and a manifestation of the wave of patriotism that culminated in the founding of Czechoslovakia in 1918. The rondo-cubist style is clearly evident on the exterior of the building, and also inside, in the decoration of the counters, walls and pillars in the main hall, and above all in the glass ceiling formed by the longitudinal intersection of three cylinders.

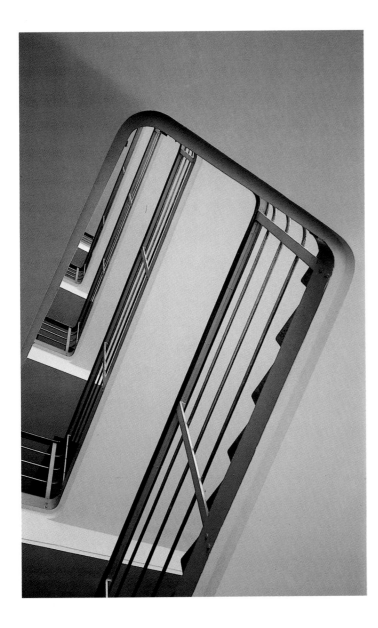

ELECTRICITY COMPANY HEADQUARTERS

Designed from 1926 to 1928 and constructed in 1935, this building is considered to be one of the finest examples of Czech avant-garde architecture from the interwar period. The designers of the Electricity Company Headquarters (Elektrické podniky), Adolf Benš and Josef Kříž, opted for a rather classic approach to the pure functionalist style of the building. The arrangement of the interior space, with its entrance halls, stairways, and both individual and collective offices, was perfectly adapted to modern administrative requirements.

VILLA TRAUB

The Villa Traub (Traubova Vila), today the headquarters for the European Commission delegation, was completed in 1929. It was designed by Bruno Paul, who was an important figure in modern German architecture and design. Paul was an influential member of the Deutscher Werkbund and director of Berlin's Kunstgewerbeschule (School of Applied Arts). Paul's architectural *oeuvre* followed a trajectory that included Art Nouveau, Art Deco and the International Style. His Villa Traub is in the purist style, a major international trend in the 1920s of which there are some particularly original examples in Prague.

MÜLLER VILLA

Designed for construction entrepreneur František Müller by Viennese architect Adolf Loos, the Müller Villa was built between 1928 and 1930. An advocate of pure functionality, Loos condemned all ornamentation in his famous article "Ornament and Crime," published in Le Corbusier's review *L'Esprit Nouveau* in 1920. His design for the Müller Villa stems from the notion of *raumplan* (spatial plan), similar to the approach adopted by Le Corbusier for a series of villas in 1922–1925. The spatial organization of the Müller Villa practically abolishes the traditional system of storeys, since the rooms are linked by a spiral-like arrangement to different levels. Despite his rationalist purism, Loos's pronounced taste for fine materials is evident in the interior decoration of the villa.

ADAM SHOP

The interior of the Adam shop (Salon Adam), formerly owned by the Knize company that specializes in luxury English menswear, was designed between 1930 and 1932 by Adolf Loos. This shop represents another example of Loos's marked taste for interiors that employ fine materials in a classic way, even when the spatial design was radically bold.

Knize opened its first shops in Vienna (1909–1913), where they still operate, and in Paris in 1927. The recent restoration and renovation of the Prague shop was carried out by the architectural firm A.D.N.S. (founded by architects Alda, Dvořák, Němec and Štempel), who also designed the Czech pavilion for Expo '92 in Seville.

Saint Wenceslas Church in Vršovice

The St. Wenceslas Church (Kostel sv. Václava), built in 1929-1930, was designed by Josef Gočár and is a masterpiece of functionalist architecture.

Functionalism was a style widespread in Prague in the 1920s and 1930s, and it led to two main trends—"scientific" functionalism and "emotive" functionalism. The "emotive" trend was developed in part by the Mánes Art Association, headed by architects Josef Gočár and Otakar Novotný. In the St. Wenceslas Church, the very function of the building called for an emphasis on the spiritual and psycho-aesthetic properties of architecture, an aspect largely ignored by "scientific" functionalism. Thus, for example, the interior layout (which perfectly corresponds to the external appearance, fulfilling one of the basic precepts of functionalism) carefully channels the flow of light toward the presbytery.

Hotel and Café Juliš

The Hotel and Café Juliš (1929–1933) on Wenceslas Square is the work of architect Pavel Janák, one of the main representatives of Czechoslovakian modernism. Janák was also one of the forerunners of cubism in architecture and the applied arts, later pioneering rondo-cubism and functionalism. This building is a highly plastic composition of pure volumes, sometimes hollow and sometimes full. Janák's bold spatial experimentation was probably inspired by Adolf Loos's theory of *raumplan*, or "spatial plan."

PRAGUE CASTLE
MODERN ADDITIONS
DESIGNED BY JOSIP PLEČNIK

In 1921, Josip Plečnik (1872–1957), a well-known architect from Slovenia who taught at Prague's School of Applied Arts, was named chief architect of Prague Castle by Tomáš Masaryk, the first president of the fledgling Czechoslovakian Republic. Among other contributions, Plečnik designed the peristyle room (1926–1928, left) which precedes the Spanish Hall, as well as the presidential wing, with its grand Roman-style impluvium (central basin). Plečnik's extraordinary sensitivity to architectonic detail and his personal vision of classical influence translate here into a remarkable harmony with the existing architecture. His enthusiasm for antiquity and his awareness of historical context also predisposed him to a sense of mutual understanding with President Masaryk. Pavel Janák, a key figure in modern Czech architecture, pointed out that, "his lot was the typical lot of modern artists—he couldn't borrow an already existing form unless he had deeply experienced it himself."

CHURCH OF THE SACRED HEART OF JESUS

Constructed between 1926 and 1932 in the Vinohrady quarter of Prague, the Church of the Sacred Heart of Jesus (Kostel Nejsvětějšího Srdce Páně) is an exceptional work by architect Josip Plečnik. Plečnik was a major figure of modernist neoclassicism and designed the church along the lines of a classical temple (originally, it was to have been surrounded by a peristyle). Plečnik's interior was also inspired by early Christian art, for example in the high altar of white marble, above which are statues of gilded wood by sculptor Damian Pešan representing Christ and six patron saints of Bohemia. Plečnik's work was highly controversial in its day, yet now appears to be a harbinger of postmodern architecture, making it seem much more contemporary and comprehensible.

Mayor's Official Reception Rooms

The ceremonial rooms (above) where the mayor (*Primator*) of Prague receives official visitors are located in the east wing of the building that houses the Municipal Library (Městská knihovna), built between 1924 and 1928 and designed by František Roith. The main staircase and rooms of the library, convey an interesting sense of space, with their Art Deco windows, walls and ceilings. The stylistic unity of the reception rooms, with their furnishings in traditional materials like wood and leather, provide an excellent example of official art during the 1920s and 1930s.

Bank of Commerce

The Bank of Commerce (Komerční banka) was designed by František Roith. Built between 1924 and 1931 (right), it is one of Roith's most important buildings in Prague from the interwar period. Others include the Ministry of Finance, the Ministry of Agriculture, the Municipal Library, and the new Bank of Commerce and Tradesmen.

Roith was a disciple of Viennese architect Otto Wagner, and became one of the main advocates of neoclassicism during the 1920s and 1930s, along with Josip Plečnik, Antonín Engel and Bohumil Hypšman. Neoclassicism became a sort of establishment style used for banks and government buildings. The Wagner school of neoclassicism effectively transposed the standard revival idiom into modern geometric structures.

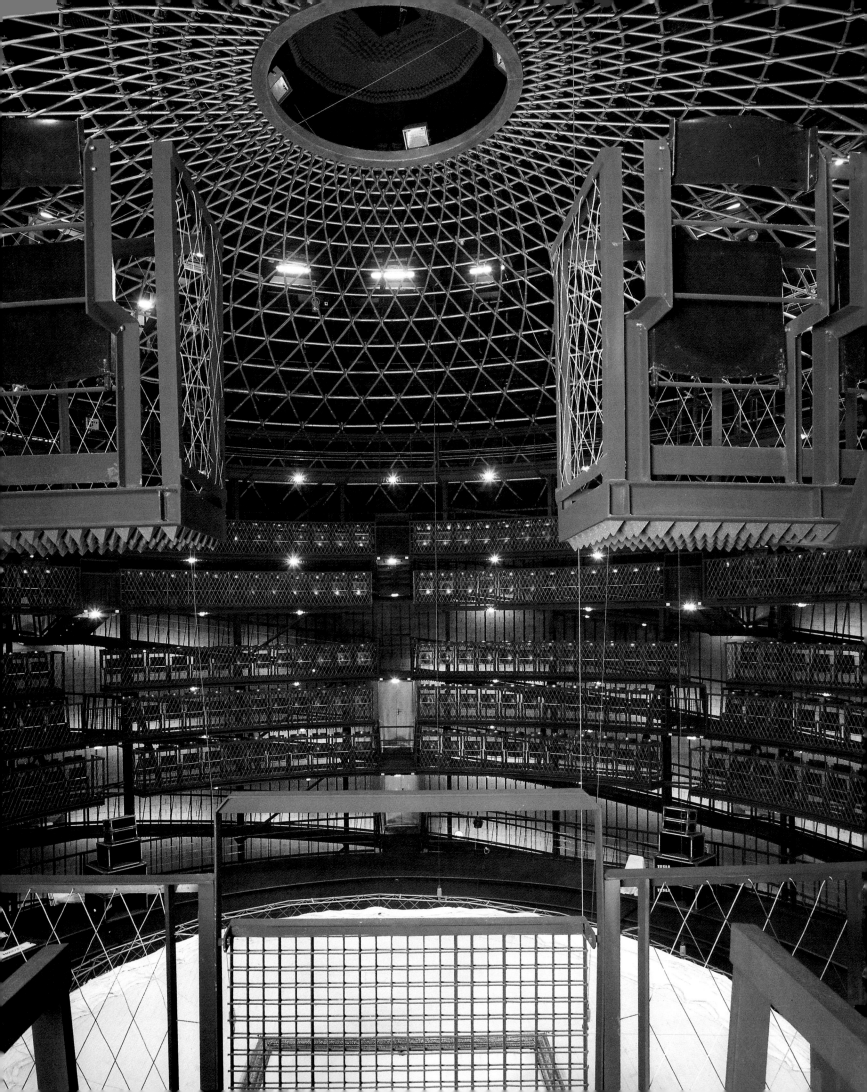

PRAGUE TODAY

LATERNA ANIMATA

A group of Prague architects who call themselves
Lo-Tech designed an imaginative high-tech theater
in the tradition of the famous Laterna Magika (Magic
Lantern) company, which pioneered multimedia
performances combining film, theater, mime and "black
theater," and attained worldwide fame during the
Universal Exposition held in Brussels in 1958.

Laterna Animata was set up in a former wide-screen movie
theater built on the site of the national exposition of 1891
that was organized in order for Bohemia to demonstrate its
economic and cultural autonomy. Laterna Animata's
technique of combining film and live actors in a "total theater
experience" was presented at the Czechoslovak pavilion at
Expo '92 in Seville.

VISITOR'S GUIDE

ROMANESQUE AND GOTHIC

CHURCH OF SAINT GEORGE

Address: Jiřské náměstí 10 (Prague Castle), Praha 1—Hradčany
Opening Times: 9 A.M. to 4 P.M. (closed Mondays).

Founded around 920 by Přemyslid Prince Vratislav, the church of St. George was enlarged when a Benedictine convent was established on the same site in 973. Following a fire in 1142, the church took on a Romanesque appearance. It underwent further modification in following centuries, but early in the twentieth century it was restored to its Romanesque form. Various features of modifications carried out during the Gothic, Renaissance and baroque periods remain, however. The convent was given a baroque facelift in the 1670s and 1680s by architect Carlo Lurago. Renovated again between 1969 and 1976, it now houses the National Gallery's collection of medieval and baroque Czech art.

ROMANESQUE HOUSE 3 U Radnice

Address: Magistrát Hlavního Města Prahy, U Radnice 3, Praha 1
Metro Station: Staroměstská
Visits upon request.

Only the ground floor (now below street level) remains of what was once a three-storey house built during the second half of the twelfth century. This was the first Romanesque house discovered in Prague during the urban renewal of the old Jewish quarter at the turn of the century. Access is via an administrative building belonging to the new Prague town hall.

HOUSE OF THE LORDS OF KUNŠTÁT

Address: Památník Jiřího z Poděbrad, Řetězová 3, Praha 1
Metro Station: Staroměstská or Můstek
Opening Times: 11 A.M. to 5 P.M. (closed Mondays).

This baronial house was constructed in the late twelfth century. During the first half of the fifteenth century, it belonged to Boček of Kunštát, uncle of George of Poděbrady (who was elected king of Bohemia in 1458 at the end of the Hussite wars). In 1846, the interior was renovated to meet the fashion for classicism, but the underlying Romanesque structure was only discovered in 1941. In 1983, it became a museum dedicated to George of Poděbrady on the occasion of the 525th anniversary of his election to the throne of Bohemia.

OLD-NEW SYNAGOGUE

Address: Červena ulice, Praha 1
Metro Station: Staroměstská
Opening Times: Daily except Saturdays, 9 A.M. to 5 P.M. in summer, 9 A.M. to 4:30 P.M. in winter.

Erected during the last quarter of the thirteenth century, this synagogue is the oldest building in Prague's Jewish quarter. The east and west façades, with their late-Gothic brick gables, date from the end of the fifteenth century and were restored in 1883 by architect Josef Mocker.

The Old-New Synagogue is one of the rare buildings remaining from the old Jewish quarter, which was leveled in 1897 during the "urban renewal" of Prague's insalubrious neighborhoods. The Jewish community has lived on this site since at least 1067, during the reign of Prince Vratislav, and made Prague a hub of Jewish culture in Europe, largely thanks to the many Hebrew printshops based there. Religious services are now being held again in the Old-New Synagogue.

SAINT MARY
OF THE SNOWS CHURCH

Address: Jungmannovo náměstí 39,
Praha 1
Metro Station: Můstek
Opening Times: Daily

Founded in 1347 by Charles IV, St. Mary of the Snows was constructed for the Carmelite convent in Prague. But the plans to make it the largest building in Prague never came to fruition. To the south of the church is a simple two-storey building belonging to the Franciscan monastery, facing the garden that serves as an oasis of greenery between Jungmann Square and Vodičkova Street.

SAINT VITUS CATHEDRAL

Address: Katedrála Svatého Víta (Prague Castle, 3rd courtyard), Praha 1 — Hradčany
Metro Station: Hradčanská or Malostranská; Tramway #22
Opening Times: 9 A.M. to 5 P.M. daily; tower open from 10 A.M. to 3 P.M. (closed Mondays).

St. Vitus Cathedral was founded in 1344 by Charles IV, and its original Gothic section is the work of French architect Matthias of Arras (died 1352) and Swabian architect Peter Parler (died 1399). Peter Parler's sons built the big south tower, but work halted with the outbreak of the Hussite wars in 1419. The choir was enclosed by a temporary wall 128 feet high. King Vladislav tried to recommence construction between 1509 and 1511, and yet another attempt to complete the cathedral was made in 1673 during the reign of Emperor Leopold I, which resulted in the laying of foundations for a baroque nave. It was only the organization of a "Union for the Completion of the Cathedral" in 1843 that ultimately terminated construction between 1873 and 1929. This final stage of building was based on designs by Josef Mocker carried out by Kamil Hilbert, giving the cathedral its current appearance.

The cathedral thus not only serves as a symbolic focus for Bohemian history (where kings are buried and the crown jewels kept), but is also a complex work of art. Inside and out, with its many chapels, the cathedral displays features of pre-Romanesque, Romanesque, Gothic, Renaissance, baroque, revival and even 1950s art. Some of the modern stained glass is the work of Alfons Mucha, the internationally-acclaimed master of Art Nouveau.

SAINT WENCESLAS CHAPEL
SAINT VITUS CATHEDRAL

Address: Katedrála Svatého Víta (Prague Castle, 3rd courtyard), Praha 1 — Hradčany
Metro Station: Hradčanská, Malostranská; Tramway #22
Opening Times: 9 A.M. to 5 P.M. daily

The chapel of St. Wenceslas was built between 1362 and 1367 by Peter Parler, the cathedral's second chief architect. It is located on the site of the south apse of the Saint Vitus rotunda founded by Prince Wenceslas in the tenth century. Dedicated to the patron saint of Bohemia, the chapel is endowed with symbolic significance. Richly decorated, it is also an example of high Gothic art under the reign of Charles IV; its square floorplan and incrustation of semi-precious stones symbolize the New Heavenly Jerusalem. Worship of St. Wenceslas, a prince of the Přemyslid dynasty, had political connotations in the eyes of Charles IV, who descended from the Přemyslids through his mother. That is also why the crown jewels are associated with this chapel.

In 1902, the agates and amethysts embedded in the chapel made a strong impression on French poet Apollinaire, who pictured himself there in the form of "a countenance with mad, flamboyant eyes." Another French writer, Paul Claudel (who was French consul in Prague between 1909 and 1911) also alluded to the door knocker in one of his *Sacred Images of Bohemia*: "Hold on, stubborn Czech! Release not that ring, Wenceslas!"

LATE GOTHIC
AND RENAISSANCE

PRAGUE CASTLE
OLD ROYAL PALACE

Address: Pražský hrad, Praha 1 — Hradčany
Metro Stations: Hradčanská, Malostranská; Tramway #22
Opening Times: 10 A.M. to 4 P.M. (closed Mondays).

The old Royal Palace is steeped in Bohemian history and displays a variety of architectural styles that reflect this tumultuous past. The Romanesque palace of Prince Soběslav I, built around 1135, was preserved underneath Vladislav Hall, which dates from 1492–1502. The Přemyslid dynasty's first Gothic palace, built over the Romanesque foundations on the orders of powerful King Ottakar II (1253–1278), was destroyed by a fire not long after completion, in 1303. A new period in the palace's history began with Charles IV of Luxembourg (1346–1378), king of Bohemia and later Holy Roman Emperor, when he returned from France in 1333 (he lived first at the court of his uncle, King Charles IV of France, then at that of his brother-in-law, Philippe VI of Valois). Charles descended from the Přemyslid line through his mother, and was determined to rebuild the palace of his ancestors. Thus he erected a two-storey "French-style" palace on the

Romanesque foundations. His son Václav IV also made a major contribution to the rebuilding of the palace even though he moved the court to Old Town in 1383.

During the Hussite wars, the palace was devastated and abandoned. It was not until 1484 that King Vladislav Jagiello took the decision to move back to the castle. He instigated numerous renovations, the most important of which were carried out by the famous architect Benedikt Ried. These included Vladislav Hall with its intricate late-Gothic vaulting, and the famous Riders' Staircase. The next stage of palace construction dates from the period following the great fire of 1541, and was the work of imperial architect Bonifác Wohlmut. It was in the Bohemian Chancellery, whose doorway bears the monogram of King Louis Jagiello, that the notorious "second defenestration of Prague" took place in 1618, when Protestant nobles threw Catholic governors Vilém Slavata and Jaroslav Martinic out the window, along with their clerk Filip Fabricius. This incident was the symbolic start of the great European conflict known as the Thirty Years' War.

Finally, during the reign of the Hapsburg empress Maria Theresa, the castle underwent major renovation between 1753 and 1774, initially directed by Italian architect Niccolo Pacassi. New wings were built in a late rococo style displaying classical influence, while the main body of the palace retained the appearance it acquired during the reigns of Vladislav and Louis Jagiello.

HVĚZDA VILLA

Address: Muzeum Aloise Jiráska a Mikoláš Aleš, letohrádek Hvězda, Praha 6 — Horní Liboc
Tramways: #1, #2 and #18; Bus #179
Opening Times: 10 A.M. to 6 P.M. (closed Mondays).

Hvězda Villa is located in the forest of Malejov, which belonged to the Břevnov monastery from the tenth century till 1534, when Emperor Ferdinand I appropriated it as a royal hunting ground. In the sixteenth century, archery contests and royal celebrations were held there. In 1620, the southwest edge of the area was the site of the last stage of the Battle of the White Mountain, in which the army of Ferdinand II of Hapsburg defeated Moravian and Silesian forces. This defeat put a tragic end to the Czech uprising yet constituted the initial stage of the Thirty Years' War. In the late eighteenth century, the hunting grounds were transformed into a landscape garden.

The villa itself was built in 1555–1556 on plans drawn up by Archduke Ferdinand of Tyrol, son of the emperor and imperial governor of Bohemia. The architects were Giovanni Maria di Pambia, Giovanni Lucchese, Bonifác Wohlmut, Hans Tirol. The upstairs banqueting hall was decorated in the seventeenth century by J. Falck, with scenes of the Battle of the White Mountain and the Thirty Years' War. These paintings were destroyed in 1783.

Under the reign of Joseph II, the villa became a powder magazine. It was restored in 1949 by the architect Pavel Janák in order to house a museum devoted to the writer Alois Jirásek, which in 1964 became the Alois Jirásek and Mikoláš Aleš Museum.

PINKAS SYNAGOGUE

Address: Entry via the old Jewish cemetary, U sarého hřbitova, Praha 1
Metro Station: Staroměstská
Opening Times: Daily except Saturdays, 9 A.M. to 5 P.M. in summer, 9 A.M. to 4:30 P.M. in winter.

Begun in 1535, the Pinkas Synagogue was originally a private synagogue belonging to the Pinkas-Horowitz family. The initial Gothic style was given a late Renaissance renovation by architect Judas of Herz in the early seventeenth century. The synagogue had originally been sandwiched between a group of houses, but the surrounding houses were demolished during urban renewal, at which point it began settling; the upstairs section has now practically sunk to street level. During the 1950s, the Pinkas Synagogue was transformed into a memorial to victims of Nazi persecution, on which painters Jiří John and Václav Boštík recorded the names of every one of the Jews of Bohemia and Moravia who died in concentration camps.

KOLOWRAT PALACE

Address: Kolovratský palác, Divadlo Kolovrat, Komorní scéna Národního divadla, Ovocny Trh 4, Praha 1
Metro Station: Můstek
Theater restaurant open Monday to Friday, 3 P.M. to midnight; Saturday and Sunday, 11 A.M. to midnight.

An early example of baroque architecture in Prague, this building's magnificent façade was erected in 1697 on plans by Giovanni Domenico Orsi from Como. Behind the palace was a vast garden and *sala terrena,* razed in 1927. The palace now houses a restaurant, café and — under the eaves — an experimental theater. It should not be confused with the other Kolowrat Palace in Malá Strana, a late baroque building that is now the official headquarters of the Ministry of Culture.

THE BAROQUE

WALLENSTEIN PALACE

Address: Ministry of Culture, Valdštejnské náměstí 4, Praha 1
Metro Station: Malostranská
Only the garden is open to the public, from May to October, 10 A.M. to 6 P.M. (closed Mondays).

This is one of the earliest examples of baroque architecture in Prague, a city still under the sway of mannerism when the palace was built between 1623 and 1630 by Italian architects. The initial architect was Andrea Spezza, who was succeeded in 1628 by Giovanni Battista Pieroni. The palace was built for Albrecht von Wallenstein, who was duke of Friedland and commander of the Imperial Catholic armies from 1625 to 1630. It was designed to reflect the power and glory of this scheming general, who secretly negotiated with the Swedes, the French, and other enemies of the Hapsburg dynasty. Wallenstein hoped to become king of Bohemia, but was sentenced to death by the emperor and assassinated by imperial officers at Cheb in 1634. Wallenstein's property was then confiscated, although part of it — including this palace — was returned to his nephew Maximilian of Wallenstein in 1639. The family lived in the residence until 1945, when it became state property. Now restored, it is used by the Ministry of Culture. The main hall and the Italianate *sala terrena* leading into the garden feature frescoes by Bartolomeo Baccio di Bianco depicting the Trojan war. Near the *sala terrena* is a grotto, called "Wallenstein's bathtub," created from artificial limestone accretions. On the other side there is a small drawing room with a fresco depicting the Argonauts and the myth of the golden fleece. In the garden and around the fountain are copies of bronze statues representing classical divinities; the originals, sculpted in 1626–1627 by Dutch sculptor Adrian de Vries, are now in Drootningholm Castle in Sweden, the Swedes having carried them off as war booty in 1648. The magnificent former riding school is now used as an exhibition venue by Prague's National Gallery.

TROJA CHÂTEAU

Address: Galerie hlavního města Prahy, U Trojského zámku, Praha 7
Metro Station: Nádraží Holešovice, Bus #112
Opening times: 10 A.M. to 6 P.M. (closed Mondays).

One of the first residences built on the outskirts of Prague, this summer château was erected in 1679–1691 for Count Václav Adalbert of Šternberk. It was designed by French architect and painter Jean-Baptiste Mathey, who designed and executed numerous

palaces and churches in Prague. Recent research suggests that architect Giovanni Domenico Orsi also largely contributed to the construction of the château up till 1685. The residence is designed along the lines of a Roman villa, adapted to the style of baroque classicism. The interior decoration was done by artists from Italy (Francesco and Giovanni Marchetti, 1689–1690) and Antwerp (Abraham and Isaak Godyn, 1690–1697).

A majestic Italianate staircase was built at the garden entrance to the château between 1685 and 1703.

The magnificent French-style formal garden is an integral part of the residence, and was laid out in 1668 by Georg Seemann.

Château and garden underwent costly restoration between 1977 and 1989 to provide the current exhibition space for the Prague Municipal Gallery's permanent collection of nineteenth-century paintings.

CLAM-GALLAS PALACE

Address: Archív hlavního města prahy, Husova 20, Praha 1
Metro Station: Staroměstská
Because of renovation, visits to the building are highly restricted and are permitted only on request.

The palace was constructed between 1713 and 1729 on the Romanesque and Gothic foundations of a residence inhabited in the fourteenth century by the margrave of Moravia, Johann Heindrich, brother of Emperor Charles IV. Designed by Viennese architect Johann Bernhard Fischer von Erlach, the current palace was built on the rather small site of the Gallas family residence, which had been confiscated from Count Wilhelm Kinsky, a friend of Wallenstein, after the latter's assassination in 1634. Count Johann Wenzel Gallas, a high imperial official who commissioned the palace, was obliged to buy several neighboring houses in order to erect his magnificent residence.

In 1757, the palace became the property of Filip von Clam, whence the current name of Clam-Gallas. Ever since a fire destroyed part of the Town Hall in Old Town in 1945, Clam-Gallas Palace has housed the municipal archives, which include major documents concerning the history of Prague from the fourteenth century to the present.

CHURCH OF SAINT NICHOLAS IN MALÁ STRANA

Address: Malostranské Náměstí, Praha 1, Malá Strana
Metro Station: Malostranská
Opening Times: 1 May to 20 September, 9 A.M. to 5 P.M.; 1 October to 30 April, 9 A.M. to 3 P.M.

St. Nicholas in Malá Strana is often considered to be Prague's finest church. It was built in stages between 1702 and 1752, first by Christoph Dientzenhofer and later by his son Kilian Ignaz. As testimony to the maturity of its designers' artistic vision, the church represents the summit of Prague baroque architecture. The main façade was completed in 1710 and is adorned with statues of the Church Fathers. The interior boasts frescoes by some of the greatest baroque artists in Prague. The

church galleries are decorated with the famous series of ten paintings depicting the Passion of Christ, executed in 1673–1674 by Karel Škréta, one of the most famous Czech baroque painters. The grand organ with its three keyboards dates from 1745–1746 and was used by Mozart during his second sojourn in Prague in 1787, when he was the guest of the Dušek family. St. Nicholas is also the church where the first requiem in honor of Mozart was celebrated in 1791.

The huge dome of St. Nicholas has become one of the most identifiable features of the Prague skyline.

CHURCH OF SAINT MARGARET BENEDICTINE MONASTERY IN BŘEVNOV

Address: Markétska 28, Praha 6 — Břevnov
Tramway: #22
Open during church services and concerts.

Founded in 993 by Bishop (later Saint) Adalbert and Prince Boleslav II, this is the oldest monastery in Bohemia. The church was dedicated to St. Benedict and St. Adalbert prior to being rededicated in the fourteenth century to St. Margaret, who was very popular at that time. The oldest archaeological remains date from the pre-Romanesque period. The church and monastery were transformed and rebuilt on several occasions, and were practically destroyed during the Hussite wars in the fifteenth century.

The baroque ensemble was constructed between 1710 and 1745, with the church being built between 1710 and 1715 and designed by Christoph Dientzenhofer and his son Kilian Ignaz. The monastic building (1709–1720), also by Christoph Dientzenhofer, is decorated with paintings executed around 1740 by Karel Kovář. The prelate's house next door features a room called the Maria Theresa Room in honor of a visit by the empress; its ceiling is decorated with a famous fresco depicting *The Miracle of the Blessed Vintíř, a Benedictine Pilgrim* (the grilled pheasant offered to Vintíř on a fast day flies away). The 1727 fresco is by Bavarian painter Cosmas Damian Asam. This is one of the most precious and best preserved frescoes in the Prague baroque style. After 1989, the monastery was returned to the Benedictine order, and in 1991 it was officially listed as a national historic monument.

ANTONÍN DVOŘÁK MUSEUM VILLA AMERIKA

Address: Ke Karlovu 20, Praha 2 — Nové Město
Metro Station: I. P. Pavlova
Opening Times: 10 A.M. to 5 P.M. (closed Mondays).

Originally a country residence, this villa was built prior to 1720 by architect Kilian Ignaz Dientzenhofer (1689–1751) on behalf of Count Jan Michna of Vacínov. The paintings were done by Johann-Ferdinand Schor (1686–1767). At the end of the eighteenth century, it was the site of a livestock market, bizarrely located in the garden containing sculptures (representing the Four Seasons) and vases from Antonín Braun's workshop.

The house has been called Villa Amerika since the later half of the nineteenth century, after the name of a restaurant formerly located nearby. In 1932, the villa became a museum devoted to the Czech composer Antonín Dvořák (1841–1904). Coincidentally, one of Dvořák's most well-known works is titled the *New World Symphony*. The museum displays manuscripts, photographs and documents tracing Dvořák's relationship with musicians such as Johannes Brahms and Hans von Bülow.

SAINT JOHN OF NEPOMUK ON THE ROCK

Address: Vyšehradská, Praha 2
Metro Station: Karlovo Náměstí
Open during Sunday church services.

The construction of the church of St. John of Nepomuk on the Rock was begun in 1730 on a design by Kilian Ignaz Dientzenhofer. The façade has a concave effect created by the interplay of two angled towers and a forward-thrusting central section. The staircase completing the façade was built from plans by architect A. Schmidt in 1776 and decorated with statues by Bernhard Otto Seeling around 1880. St. John of Nepomuk, canonized in 1729 was

extremely popular during the baroque period and became one of the country's patron saints. According to a legend perpetuated by the Jesuits, he died as a martyr to the secrecy of confession — for refusing to report what the queen had confessed, King Václav IV had him tortured and thrown into the Vltava from the Charles Bridge.

FORMER MONASTERY IN ZBRASLAV

Address: Národní Galerie v Praze, sbírka českého sochařství XIX a XX století, zámek Zbraslav, Praha 5
Metro Station: Smíchovské nádraží, then Bus #129, #241, #243 or #255
The former monastery can also be reached by boats going up the Vltava River (departing from Palacký Bridge landing).
Opening Times: 10 A.M. to 6 P.M. (closed Mondays).

A Cistercian monastery was founded in Zbraslav in 1292 by King Václav II, but the order's most magnificent edifice — the grandest in the kingdom of Bohemia — was destroyed in 1420 during the Hussite wars. The monastery was restored in the second half of the fifteenth century only to fall victim to the Thirty Years' War. It was not until the early eighteenth century that the monastery underwent a second

period of glory. The monastery and prelate's house were built between 1709 and 1739 on designs by architect Giovanni Santini-Aichel (1667–1723) and his disciple and colleague František Maxmilián Kaňka (1674–1766), who practiced a revival style known as "baroque Gothic." The frescoes in the interior are the work of Václav Vavřinec Reiner (1689–1743) and F. X. Palko (1724–1767). The monastery was disbanded during the reforms imposed by Emperor Joseph II in 1785—soon after it became a sugar refinery and later a chemical factory.

The monastery buildings, constituting precious examples of Bohemian baroque architecture, fortunately escaped devastation thanks to the purchase of the estate by Cyril Bartoň of Dobenín in 1910. In 1942, Bartoň placed the site at the disposal of the National Gallery. The buildings now house the Gallery's collection of Czech sculpture from the nineteenth and twentieth centuries.

Ownership of the Zbraslav château has now been restored to the Bartoň family, and the National Gallery rents its exhibition space for a symbolic sum of money.

KLEMENTINUM

Address: Mariánské náměstí 5, Praha 1
Metro Station: Staroměstská
Opening Times: Monday to Saturday, 8 A.M. to 7 P.M.; certain departments have special opening times.
The Chapel of Mirrors is open only for concerts and exhibitions.

The Jesuits were summoned to Bohemia in 1556 by Emperor Ferdinand I, who wanted them to assist in the Counter-Reformation. They first moved into the former Dominican monastery of Sv. Kliment (St. Clement), from which the name for this vast complex of religious and secular buildings was taken. The construction of this masterpiece of architecture and interior decoration

stretched over nearly 150 years, until the Jesuit order was expelled in 1773. The Klementinum subsequently housed the diocesan seminary, plus the library and lecture halls for Charles University. The first public art gallery opened there in 1796 and in 1800 the Academy of Fine Arts moved in. After 1923, the Klementinum became the site of the national and university libraries, and was renovated for this purpose by architect Ladislav Machoň, with the collaboration of artists such as sculptor Otto Gutfreund. The Klementinum currently houses the National Library of the Czech Republic, divided into National Library, Slavic Library, Technical Library, and University Library (which houses the department of rare manuscripts).

THUN PALACE
BRITISH EMBASSY

Address: Thunoská 14, Praha 1
Metro Station: Malostranská

Initially the Renaissance residence of the counts of Leslie, the building was bought sometime after 1656 by the archbishop of Salzburg, Quidobald Thun-Hohenstein. It was given a baroque face-lift between 1716 and 1727, probably based on plans by architect Giovanni Battista Alliprandi (1665–1720).

BUQUOY PALACE
FRENCH EMBASSY

Address: Velkopřevorské náměstí 2, Praha 1
Metro Station: Malostranská

This palace was built in two stages, in 1719 and in 1735, and was probably designed by architect František Maxmilián Kaňka, considered a successor of Giovanni Santini-Aichel. It was substantially renovated during the latter half of the nineteenth century. The palace belonged to the Buquoy family from 1748 to the time of the first Czechoslovak Republic

(1918–1938), and later became the French Embassy.

AT THE GOLDEN GOOSE
STERNEGG PALACE

A private residence in Malá Strana, the Sternegg Palace is not open to the public. For security reasons, the owners prefer to keep the address private.

CLASSICISM AND REVIVAL STYLES

ESTATES THEATER

Address: Železná 11, Praha 1
Metro Station: Můstek
Guided Visits: Saturdays and Sundays, every half hour from 9 A.M. to 11 A.M., or upon request.

Financed by Count Nostitz-Rhienek, the neoclassic opera house dates from 1781–1783. The architect was Anton Haffenecker, and the interior decoration was the work of Jan Quirin Jahn and Josef Bergler (the first director of Prague's Academy of Fine Arts). On the façade is the lion of Bohemia and a Latin inscription, *Patriae et Musis*. The theater was called the Nostitz Theater until it was acquired by the Estates of Bohemia (the regional assembly) in 1799, at which point it became known as the Estates Theater (Stavovské divadlo).

Almost all performances at the theater were in German until 1920, when Czech actors, impatient with the lack of a governmental decision, began performing in Czech. The theater was then administratively attached to the National Theater and was renamed the Tyl Theater in 1949.

The building has undergone several renovations and restorations, which seriously undermined its stylistic purity. The extensive and costly restoration recently carried out was designed to return it to its original state

as far as possible, all the while enabling the theater to meet current artistic needs. Once again named the Estates Theater, it is famous for its performances of Mozart's operas.

In 1834, during the premiere of a piece by Czech playwright Josef Kajetán Tyl, a song titled "Where is My Homeland?" rang out—a song that would later become world-renowned as the Czech national anthem.

FORMER VÁVRA HOUSE
POST OFFICE MUSEUM

Address: Nové Mlýny 2, Praha 1
Metro Station: náměstí Republiky
Opening Times: 9 A.M. to 5 P.M. (closed Mondays).

Vávra House was originally a mill, a reminder that there were water mills on the banks of the Vltava from the fourteenth century until 1916 (the house, moreover, is located on New Mill Street). Since 1988, Vávra House has been the home of the Post Office Museum, founded in 1918. The museum traces the development of postal services and telecommunications in former Czechoslovakia, and has a particularly interesting collection of European stamps.

SPANISH SYNAGOGUE

Address: Dušni ulice 12, Praha 1
Metro Station: Staroměstská
Opening Times: Daily except Saturdays, 9 A.M. to 5 P.M. in summer, 9 A.M. to 4:30 P.M. in winter.

The pseudo-Moorish Spanish Synagogue was built in the 1860s and designed by architects Ignác Ullman and Josef Niklas. The current synagogue, covered by a dome, displays a composite style containing Moorish and Renaissance elements. The interior is richly decorated with a profusion of stucco and gilding.

The synagogue now houses a rich collection of embroidered textiles used in synagogues as far back as the sixteenth century, such as tabernacle curtains, mantelets for the Torah, and rugs to cover pulpits.

NATIONAL THEATER

Address: Národní třída 4, Praha 1
Metro Station: Národní
Guided Visits: Saturdays and Sundays, every half-hour from 8 A.M. to 11 A.M., or upon request.

The original neo-Renaissance theater, designed by Josef Zítek, was built between 1868 and 1881, when it was damaged in a fire. Josef Schulz oversaw the repairs and the theater reopened on 18 November 1883. Between 1977 and 1983, the theater was renovated, and the Nová Scéna wing added. The chariots with Goddesses of Victory on the main façade are by sculptor Bohuslav Schnirch (1910–1911). On the façade overlooking the river is a portal with statues representing Opera and Drama, done in 1874 by Josef Václav Myslbek (1848–1922), the father of modern Czech sculpture. The National Theater hosts performances of Czech and foreign operas, plays, and ballets.

NATIONAL MUSEUM

Address: Václavské náměstí 68, Praha 2
Metro Station: Muzeum
Opening Times: 9 A.M. to 5 P.M. (closed Mondays).

Architect Josef Schulz executed this neo-Renaissance edifice between 1885 and 1890. The museum was built on the upper end of Václavské náměstí (Wenceslas Square) where the classical-style Horse Gate had stood until 1875 (the square was originally the site of a horse market). The monumental design and organization of Schulz's exterior was inspired by Gottfried Semper and Karl von Hasenauer's Hofburg Museum in Vienna. The main entrance ramp is adorned with allegorical statues by Antonín Wagner. They represent Bohemia, Moravia and Silesia (the three regions of the former kingdom of Bohemia), as well as the Elbe and the Vltava, the country's two main rivers. The building suffered damage several times in the course of the twentieth century, notably during the Prague uprising against the Nazis in May 1945 and the Soviet invasion of August 1968. The most serious damage, however, was probably done by the absurd decision to build Prague's major north-south artery just in front of the museum, an error compounded by making the site a transit hub in the form of a subway interchange.

Initially, the museum collection was devoted mainly to the natural sciences. It now includes a wealth of literary items, mainly ancient manuscripts and musicological documents, as well as displays on prehistory, numismatics, weaponry (notably from the Hussite wars), archaeology, mineralogy, zoology, geology and paleontology. On an institutional level, the National Museum is composed of thirteen separate departments, some of which are housed elsewhere.

RUDOLFINUM

Address: nám J. Palacha 1, Praha 1
Metro Station: Staroměstská

Designed by architects Josef Zítek and Josef Schulz, this neo-Renaissance edifice was constructed between 1876 and 1884. It was named the Rudolfinum in honor of Archduke Rudolf, and was initially a concert hall and exhibition space. After the Czechoslovak Republic was founded in 1918, it was used as the nation's parliament. It became a concert hall once again in 1943, and was renamed the House of Artists (Dům umělců) when it became the headquarters for the National Conservatory of Music and the Academy of Musical Arts. After major renovations recently carried out by architect Karel Prager, the Rudolfinum has been restored to its original function.

CZECH SAVINGS BANK

Address: Cěská spořitelna, Rytířská 29, Praha 1
Metro Station: Můstek
Opening Times: Monday to Friday 8 A.M. to 6 P.M., Saturday 8:30 A.M. to 12:30 P.M.

The building that housed the former Municipal Savings Bank was erected between 1892 and 1894 in a Palladio-inspired neo-Renaissance style by architects Antonín Wiehl (1846–1910) and Osvald Polívka (1859–1931). The façade is decorated with figures thematically linked to the concept of savings, executed by a group of artists that included Stanislav Sucharda (a major artist of the Czech Secession school). In 1953, the building was transformed into a museum dedicated to Klement Gottwald (1896–1953), a participant in the 1948 "Prague coup" who became the country's first Communist president. The museum displayed documents relating to the history of the Czech Communist Party. After 1989, the building was restored to its original function.

STATE OPERA
FORMER SMETANA THEATER

Address: Wilsonova 8, Praha 1
Metro Station: Muzeum

At the initiative of Prague's German community, the theater was constructed in 1886–1888 by architect M. Wertmüller and designed by Viennese duo Ferdinand Fellner and Hermann Helmer. Between 1967 and 1973, it was restored and enlarged. The allegorical chariots of Dionysus and Thalia on the façade are the work of sculptor T. Friedel. Originally called the New German Theater (because performances were in German), it was briefly dubbed the Grand Opera of May 5th (in honor of the Prague uprising against the Germans in 1945). It became the Smetana Theater in 1950 when it was made an administrative part of the National Theater and is now known as the State Opera.

U KORUNY PHARMACY

Address: Malé náměstí 13, Praha 1
Metro Station: Staroměstská
Opening Times: Monday to Friday, 9 A.M. to 4 P.M.

Given a neo-baroque facelift in 1889, this Gothic house is home to one of the oldest pharmacies in Prague. On the façade is a gilded crown that lent its name to the building (At the Crown).

BANK OF COMMERCE
AND TRADESMEN

Address: Živnostenska Banka, Na příkopě 20, Praha 1
Metro Station: Můstek or náměstí Republiky
Opening Times: 8 A.M. to 5 P.M.

Built in 1894–1896 by architect Osvald Polívka, the bank's façade features allegorical statues representing Technology, Agriculture, Industry and Commerce at the mezzanine level, medallions containing allegorical mosaics (based on cartoons by Mikoláš Aleš) under the cornice, and floral patterns along the attic level.

ART NOUVEAU
AND THE BEGINNINGS
OF MODERNISM

MAIN TRAIN STATION

Address: Wilsonova, Praha 1
Metro Station: Hlavní nádraží

Prague's main train station was built between 1900 and 1909. The design by architect Josef Fanta (1856–1954) replaced a neo-Renaissance building designed by Antonín Barvitius in 1870. The decoration of the new station was confided to major Prague artists of the day, such as sculptor Stanislav Sucharda, Ladislav Šaloun, and Čeněk Vosmík. The interior paintings are the work of Václav Jansa. The modernization of the station and construction of a large hall linking it to the subway, undertaken between 1972 and 1977, did not alter the older sections, which is why the station is now officially listed as a historical monument.

HOTEL EVROPA

Address: Václavské náměstí 25, Praha 1
Metro Station: Můstek
Opening Times (restaurant and café): Daily, 7 A.M. to 12 midnight.

The Hotel Evropa (comprising the former Hotels Archduke Stefan and Garni) was built between 1903 and 1905 by architects Bedřich Bendelmayer (1872–1932) and Alois Dryák (1872–1932) in Secession style with floral decorative motifs.

CZECH NATIONAL INSURANCE BANK

Address: Česká státní pojišťovna, Spálená 14, Praha 1
Metro Station: Můstek
Opening Times: Monday to Friday, 8 A.M. to 12 P.M. and 1 P.M. to 3 P.M.; Saturdays and Sundays, 9 A.M. to 2 P.M.

The architect Osvald Polívka (1859–1931) designed this building

which dates from 1907–1909. Polívka was initially a partisan of the neo-Renaissance style, as seen in the former Municipal Savings Bank and the former Zemská bank (both illustrated in this book); he then designed buildings in the Secession style, such as the Praha insurance building.

BANK OF COMMERCE

Address: Komerční banka, Na příkopě 3, Praha 1
Metro Station: Můstek
Opening Times: Monday to Friday, 8 A.M. to 11 A.M. and 1 P.M. to 6 P.M.

This 1906–1908 building formerly housed the Union of Viennese Banks (Wiener Bankverein) and was designed by German architect Josef Zasche (1871–1957), who was a disciple of neo-Renaissance Viennese architect Karl von Hasenauer. Zasche became a leading representative of the neoclassic trend in modern architecture, and was president of the Association of German Architects in Czechoslovakia.

JUBILEE SYNAGOGUE

Address: Jeruzalemská 7, Praha 1
Metro Station: Hlavní nádraží
Open during services on Friday evening and Saturday.

The Jubilee Synagogue, located in Prague's New Town (Nové Město) was constructed in 1905–1906 on a Moorish-style design by Wilhelm Stiastny and Alois Richter.

LUCERNA PALACE

Address: Štěpánská 61, Praha 1 — Vodičkova 36, Praha 1
Metro Station: Muzeum or Můstek

Designed by architect Václav Havel, the Lucerna Palace was built in two stages between 1907 and 1918. A multipurpose complex, it comprises a passage between Štěpánská and Vodičkova Streets that serves as a shopping arcade complete with movie theater, conventional theater, and reception hall for dances and concerts.

MUNICIPAL HOUSE

Address: náměstí Republiky 5, Praha 1
Metro Station: náměstí Republiky
Opening Times: Café, 7 A.M. to 11 P.M.; French restaurant, 11 A.M. to 11 P.M.; Pilsen restaurant, which serves the famous Pilsner Urquell 12 beer, 12 A.M. to 4 P.M. (closed Sundays).

Designed in 1903 by architects Antonín Balšánek and Osvald Polívka and built in 1905–1912, the Municipal House was erected next to the famous fifteenth-century Powder Tower, where the royal court once stood. Despite its stylistic eclecticism, the building is generally considered one of the finest examples of Czech Art Nouveau (known as Secession style).

ALFONS MUCHA'S HOUSE

Address: Hradčanské náměstí 6, Praha 1
Metro Station: Malostranská or Hradčanská
This house still belongs to the Mucha family and is not open to the public.

Alfons Mucha lived in an old house located on Hradčanské náměstí (Castle Square) at the corner of Kanovnická Street, to the right of Toscana Palace (just across a narrow alley). The house was built in 1414 for a canon, Václav of Radeč, who was supervising construction of the cathedral. In 1486, the house was redecorated by the prevost, Hanuš of Kolowrat. It was originally an isolated building with a residential wing and a tower that can still be seen at the southwestern corner. It underwent baroque renovation in 1685 and was altered again in 1734, probably by the architect A. V. Spannbrucker. Mucha moved into the house in 1910.

HOUSE AND STUDIO OF SCULPTOR STANISLAV SUCHARDA

Address: Slavíčkova 6, Praha 6 — Bubeneč
Not open to the public.

Designed by Jan Kotěra (1871–1923), the father of modern Czech architecture, this house was constructed between 1905 and 1907 for sculptor Stanislav Sucharda (1886–1916). Sucharda taught at the School of Applied Arts and later at Prague's Academy of Fine Arts, and was a major figure in the art movement known as the Czech Secession. He executed the large monument to the historian František Palacký, and is also known for remarkable reliefs and medallions.

HOUSE OF PUBLISHER JAN LAICHTER

Address: Editio Supraphon Hudební nakladatelství, Chopinova 4, Praha 2 — Vinohrady
Metro Station: Jiřího z Poděbrad
Not open to the public.

Architect Jan Kotěra designed this residence, constructed in 1908–1909. Kotěra studied under Otto Wagner in Vienna before becoming a professor in Prague, first at the School of Applied Arts and later at the Academy of Fine Arts. He initially developed a type of "floral modernism," then became one of the most fervent advocates of geometric modernism.

FRANTIŠEK BÍLEK MUSEUM

Address: Galerie hlavního města Prahy, Mickiewiczova 1, Praha 6
Metro Station: Hradčanská or Malostranská
Opening Times: 10 A.M. to 6 P.M. (closed Mondays).
František Bílek's studio is open from May 15th to October 15th.

The symbolist sculptor František Bílek (1872–1941) designed this studio-house himself. Inspired by Dutch and Anglo–American architecture, the segmented building is of red brick. In 1963, the artist's widow bequeathed villa, studio and all contents to Prague's Municipal Gallery. In front of the façade is the sculpture of *Comenius Saying Farewell to His Country*.

FORMER FESTIVAL CLUB

Address: Václavské náměstí 26, Praha 1
Metro Station: Muzeum or Můstek

Architect Matěj Blecha designed the Secession-style bar in 1912. It was installed in the basement of a late eighteenth-century baroque residence.

PRELATE'S HOUSE MONASTERY OF ZBRASLAV

Address: zámek Zbraslav, Praha 5
Metro Station: Smíchovské nádraží, then bus #129, #241, #243, or #255
The monastery can also be reached by boat (departing from Palacký Bridge landing). Visits upon request.

The prelate's house of the former Cistercian monastery in Zbraslav is the product of the reconstruction of a Gothic building, carried out by architect František Maxmilián Kaňka prior to 1739. It was again renovated in 1911–1912 by architect Dušan Jurkovič (1868–1947), at the initiative of Cyril Bartoň of Dobenín. On the second floor is a cycle of paintings by Václav Vavřinec Reiner depicting episodes from the monastery's history.

NA LIBUŠINCE HOUSE

Address: Rašínovo nábřeží 26, Praha 2
Metro Station: Karlovo náměstí; Tramway: #17
Not open to the public.

Designed by architect Emil Králíček (1877–1930), this house was built sometime after 1912. Králíček belonged to the Czech school of cubist architecture. He studied in Darmstadt under the famous German architect Joseph Maria Olbrich, then worked in Prague for a number of architectural firms. The most active of these was Matěj Blecha's office, one of the first to execute cubist designs. Králíček was responsible for one of the most emblematic symbols of Prague architecture, the famous 1912 cubist street lamp on Jungmann Square; he also constructed the Diamond House on Spálená Street.

THE 1920s AND 1930s

BANK OF THE CZECHOSLOVAK LEGIONS

Address: Česká obchodní banka, Na poříčí 24, Praha 1
Metro Station: náměstí Republiky
Opening Times: Monday to Friday, 7 A.M. to 3 P.M.

Typical of the so-called "national style," also known as rondo-cubism, the bank was built between 1921 and 1923 and designed by Josef Gočár (1880–1945). He was the first president, in 1911, of the cubist-oriented "Group of Fine Artists" as well as being a major figure of modern Czech architecture. He was an exponent of cubism, rondo-cubism and functionalism, and also played an important role as town planner. To decorate the façade of this building, Gočár called on two of the most important Czech sculptors of the day, Josef Štursa (who sculpted the capitals) and Otto Gutfreund.
  Gutfreund's friezes illustrate the story of the Czechoslovak legions, which were founded in 1917 to fight for Czechoslovakian independence from the Austro-Hungarian Empire. The legions fought until the end of the war on various fronts, notably in Russia where they clashed with the Bolsheviks and temporarily seized control of the Trans-Siberian Railroad.
  The bank is now known as the Czech Bank of Commerce.

ELECTRICITY COMPANY HEADQUARTERS

Address: Bubenská 1, Praha 7 — Holešovice
Metro Station: Vlatavska or nádraží Holešovice; Tramway #17

This key example of Prague functionalist architecture was built in 1935 based on designs drawn up from 1926 to 1928 by Adolf Benš (1894–1982) and Josef Kříž. Benš was a disciple of Jan Kotěra and Josef Gočár, taught at Prague's School of Applied Arts, and was named a member of the Paris Architecture Academy in 1964.

VILLA TRAUB

Address: Pod hradbami 17, Praha 6
Metro Station: Hradčanská or Dejvická; Tramway #18

This example of the purist style was built from 1928 to 1929 based on a design by German architect Bruno Paul (1874–1968). Paul was an active member of the Deutscher Werkbund who hoped to revamp architecture and design; in 1906 he was appointed director of the Kunstgewerbeschule (School of Applied Arts) in Berlin. He had exhibited his famous Hunting Room —typical of the German school of Art Nouveau, called Jugendstil—and was also behind the concept of simple, standardized furniture (*Typenmöbel*) that would enhance the quality of mass-produced furniture.

MÜLLER VILLA

Address: Nad hradním vodojemem 14, Praha 6 — Střešovice
Metro Station: Hradčanská; Tramway #18
Not open to the public.

Adolf Loos (1870–1933), father of purism and functionalism, designed this house in association with architect Karel Lhota for the entrepreneur František Müller. Loos became a Czechoslovakian citizen in 1930 and designed other projects for Prague; he helped introduce functionalist ideas into Czech architecture.

ADAM SHOP

Address: Na příkopě 8, Praha 1
Metro Station: Můstek
Opening Times: Monday to Friday, 9 A.M. to 7 P.M.; Saturday, 9 A.M. to 1 P.M.

The interior of this shop for the Knize menswear firm was designed by Adolf Loos between 1930 and 1932.

SAINT WENCESLAS CHURCH IN VRŠOVICE

Address: Naměstí Svatopluka Čecha, Praha 2 — Vršovice
Metro Station: náměstí Míru, then Tramway #4 or #22

Built from 1929 to 1930 from designs by Josef Gočár (1880–1945), the church is an example of "emotive" functionalism. The high altar's cross and relief of the Patron Saints of Bohemia are by C. Vosmík. The altar of the Virgin Mary is by K. Pokorný, while J. Kubiček executed the altar of the Sacred Heart of Jesus and the relief on Saint Joseph's altar. The Stations of the Cross are by B. Stefan and the front stained-glass window is based on a cartoon by J. Kaplický.

HOTEL AND CAFE JULIŠ

Address: Václavské náměstí 22, Praha 1
Metro Station: Můstek
Café Opening Times: Daily from 9 A.M. to 7:30 P.M.

This major example of functionalism was built between 1929 and 1933 by architect Pavel Janák (1882–1956), a follower of the Viennese architect Otto Wagner. In 1911, Janák was one of the founding members of cubist-oriented "Group of Fine Artists," later becoming a representative of the "national style." He taught at the School of Applied Arts and was appointed head architect of Prague Castle in 1936. An influential teacher, Janák was one of the most important theorists of Czech architecture.

PRAGUE CASTLE
MODERN ADDITIONS DESIGNED BY JOSIP PLEČNIK

Address: Pražský hrad, Praha 1 — Hradčany
Metro Stations: Hradčanská, Malostranská; Tramway #22
Partly open to the public on certain days (which may vary).

Born in Ljubljana, Josip Plečnik (1872–1957) studied with Otto Wagner at the Academy of Fine Arts in Vienna. There he met Jan Kotěra, a key figure in modern Czech architecture. Plečnik won the Vienna Academy's Rome scholarship, which enabled him to study the ancient architecture that would influence his work. Between 1911 and 1921, he taught at the School of Applied Arts in Prague. In 1920 he was appointed chief architect of Prague Castle by President Tomáš Masaryk. The renovations that Plečnik carried out in Prague Castle

constitute the main courtyard, the peristyle room, the presidential apartments, the garden on the bastion, the third courtyard, the Paradise garden, and the garden on the ramparts. Classical elements such as pillars, obelisks, pergolas and fountains, create a sacred area around the castle, recalling temples in antiquity. In this respect, his style might be described as modernist neoclassic architecture.

CHURCH OF THE SACRED HEART OF JESUS

Address: náměstí Jiřího z Poděbrad, Praha 2 — Vinohrady
Metro Station: Jiřího z Poděbrad
The church is open during religious services.

Built between 1926 and 1932, the church of the Sacred Heart of Jesus (Nejsvětějšího Srdce Páně) was designed by Josip Plečnik. The church portals are decorated with sculptures by Bedřich Stefan.

MAYOR'S OFFICIAL RECEPTION ROOMS

Address: Mariánské náměstí
Metro Station: Staroměstská
Opening Times: 10 A.M. to 6 P.M. (closed Mondays).

These rooms are located in the east wing of the building that houses the Municipal Library, built between 1924 and 1928 and designed in a neoclassic style by František Roith, a former student of Otto Wagner, and a key representative of 1920s neoclassicism, which became an official style for public buildings and major banks. The main façade is decorated with six allegorical figures by sculptor Ladislav Kofránek (1928). The third floor of the library building will also house the National Gallery's collection of twentieth-century Czech paintings during the renovation of the Trade Fair building.

BANK OF COMMERCE

Address: Václavské náměstí 42-44-46, Praha 1
Metro Station: Muzeum
Opening Times: Monday to Friday, 9 A.M. to 11 A.M. and 1 P.M. to 6 P.M.

Built between 1924 and 1931, the bank was designed by František Roith (1876–1942), a follower of Otto Wagner and advocate of neoclassicism in the 1920s and 1930s.

LATERNA ANIMATA

Address: Výstaviště, Praha 7
Metro Station: Nádraží Holešovice; Tramways #5, #12, #17

This theater was built between 1991 and 1992 in a former wide-screen movie theater. It was designed by architects Jindřich Smetana, Tomáš Kulík, Jan Louda, and Zbyněk Stýblo from Lo-Tech Design Studio in Prague.

INDEX